THE
NATIVE AMERICAN
STRUGGLE
IN UNITED STATES HISTORY

★ IN ★
UNITED STATES
★ HISTORY ★

ANITA
★ LOUISE ★
McCORMICK

Enslow Publishers, Inc.
40 Industrial Road
Box 398
Berkeley Heights, NJ 07922
USA

http://www.enslow.com

Originally published as *Native Americans and the Reservation in American History* in 1996.

No part of this book may be reproduced by any means without the written permission of the publisher.

Library of Congress Cataloging-in-Publication Data

McCormick, Anita Louise.
  [Native Americans and the reservation in American history]
  The Native American struggle in United States history / Anita Louise McCormick.
    pages cm. — (In United States history)
  "Originally published as Native American and the Reservation In American History in 1996."
  Includes bibliographical references and index.
  ISBN 978-0-7660-6325-9
  1. Indian reservations—History—Juvenile literature. 2. Indians of North America—Government relations—Juvenile literature. 3. Indians of North America—Land tenure—Juvenile literature. I. Title.
  E91.M24 2015
  323.1197—dc23
                                                    2014025746
Printed in the United States of America

102014 Bang Printing, Brainerd, Minn.

10 9 8 7 6 5 4 3 2 1

Future Editions:
Paperback ISBN: 978-0-7660-6326-6
EPUB ISBN: 978-0-7660-6327-3
Single-User PDF ISBN: 978-0-7660-6328-0
Multi-User PDF ISBN: 978-0-7660-6329-7

To Our Readers: We have done our best to make sure all Internet addresses in this book were active and appropriate when we went to press. However, the author and the publisher have no control over and assume no liability for the material available on those Internet sites or on other Web sites they may link to. Comments can be sent by e-mail to comments@enslow.com or to the address on the back cover.

♻ Enslow Publishers, Inc., is committed to printing our books on recycled paper. The paper in every book contains 10% to 30% post-consumer waste (PCW). The cover board on the outside of each book contains 100% PCW. Our goal is to do our part to help young people and the environment too!

Illustration Credits: ©Thinkstock/iStock/Mark Hammon, p. 4; ©Thinkstock/iStock/R_Litewriter, p. 1; Enslow Publishers, Inc., p. 37; United States Bureau of the Census-1990, p. 79.

Cover Illustration: ©Thinkstock/iStock/R_Litewriter
Cover Caption: This Native American elder is performing a traditional tribal dance.

☆ CONTENTS ☆

A teepee constructed in the southwest United States. Native Americans experienced many difficulties maintaining their traditional ways of life as the United States expanded.

Chapter 1

THIS LAND WAS THEIR LAND

The church in Omaha, Nebraska, where Standing Bear had been invited to tell his story, was overflowing with people. Many had read the article in the local newspaper about the mistreatment of Standing Bear and his tribe, the Ponca, by United States government agents. Now, on this fall day of 1879, they had come to hear his story for themselves.

Standing Bear first related the story of his people. The Ponca, he told the congregation, were a peaceful tribe that lived in Nebraska near the bank of the Missouri River. They raised corn and other vegetables on their farms. They were eager to trade with white settlers and had never been at war with the United States government.

Then one day, in January 1877, government agents came. "The inspector said to us: The President says you must sell this land. He will buy it and pay you the money, and give you new land in Indian Territory," Standing Bear told the congregation.[1] "We said to him: 'We do not know your authority. You have no right to move us till we have had council with the President.'"[2]

After much discussion with the chiefs, the agents made a proposal. They wanted all ten Ponca chiefs to go with them by train and see the reservation that the government had set aside for them in Indian Territory, an area known today as Oklahoma.

Once they saw it, the chiefs would be permitted to report back to the president and let him know if the land was a suitable place for their tribe to live.

The Government Agents' Deceit

But once the chiefs arrived in Indian Territory, the agents kept none of their promises. First, the agents refused to pay any money for the Ponca tribe's ancestral homeland. "You have forgotten what you said before we started," Standing Bear told the agent. "You said we should have pay for our land."[3]

And that was only the beginning of the agents' deceit. All three pieces of land the agents showed the Ponca chiefs were far inferior to the rich, fertile farmland the tribe lived on in Nebraska. The soil was rocky and the few trees that grew there were short and scrubby. The land was totally unsuitable for farming.

"We do not like this land," Standing Bear told the agents. "We could not support ourselves. The water is bad. Now send us to Washington, to tell the President, as you promised."[4]

But the agents refused, saying, "The President did not tell me to take you to Washington; neither did he tell me to take you home."[5] Now all ten Ponca chiefs were stranded several hundred miles from their home with very little money and no supplies.

The agents even took away the interpreter, whom the chiefs had paid, and would not show them the way back to the railroad. "He left us right there," Standing Bear said:

> It was winter. We started for home on foot. . . . We barely lived till morning, it was so cold. We had nothing but our blankets. We took the ears of corn that had dried in the fields; we ate it raw. The soles of our moccasins wore out.

We were barefoot in the snow. We were nearly dead when we reached the Otoe Reserve.[6]

By then, the Ponca chiefs had been walking for fifty days. They stayed with the Otoes for several days to regain their strength. When they left to continue their journey home, the Otoes gave each chief a pony to ride.

But before the chiefs were able to make their way home, the government agents returned to the Ponca homeland with soldiers and ordered the tribe to move to Indian Territory. No one wanted to leave. The Poncas demanded that the chiefs be returned before any decision was made. But even after the chiefs found their way back home, they could do nothing to stop the agents and soldiers from forcing the Ponca people off their land.

The government soldiers took all the Ponca's farming tools and household furniture and put them into a big building. They threw all the Ponca's smaller possessions into a wagon. Then they forced the Ponca tribe to move at gunpoint. "We told them that we would rather die than leave our lands; but we could not help ourselves. They took us down. Many died on the road. Two of my children died. After we reached the new land, all my horses died. The water was very bad. All our cattle died; not one was left,"[7] Standing Bear said.

The congregation was shocked at what they heard. Many people were inspired to write letters to Congress and protest the unfair treatment the Ponca tribe had received at the hands of government agents.

Standing Bear continued to travel and speak about what happened to him and his tribe. Because of Standing Bear's efforts, many white Americans began to realize how poorly Native Americans were being treated. Not all of the tribes that the government relocated to Indian Territory were treated as badly as the Ponca. But few Native American chiefs had willingly agreed to give up their ancestral homeland and relocate their tribe to land that America's white government had "reserved" for them. In many cases, they had been lied to, cheated, threatened, or otherwise forced to move against their will. That was the real story of the removal of Native Americans to reservations.

Beliefs about Land Ownership

Before European settlers arrived in North America, this entire continent was inhabited by many diverse tribes of Native Americans. Each tribe spoke a language that was unique to its people. Every tribe had its own culture, religion, ceremonies, and ways of providing food. Some Native American tribes lived primarily through their farming skills. Other tribes specialized in hunting, gathering, fishing, or trading. Their methods of building shelters and homes differed as well. Native Americans belonging to some tribes lived in tepees, while others lived in log homes or houses made of earthen bricks.

Religion was central to every Native American culture. It was the heart of their being. Every tribe had its own religion and its own ways of honoring the creator, or Great Spirit. Nearly all tribes believed that animals, plants, and even the earth held a certain spiritual significance. And they believed that the Great Spirit had placed their tribe where it had for a special purpose.

Arapoosih, a leader of the Crow tribe of Montana during the nineteenth century, expressed this sentiment:

> The Crow country is a good country. The Great Spirit put it exactly in the right place; while you are in it you fare well; whenever you are out of it, whichever way you travel, you fare worse. . . . The Crow country is in exactly in the right place. Everything good is to be found there. There is no place like Crow country.[8]

Every tribe knew the land they lived on better than any other. As a result, they were acutely aware of the many wonderful resources the land offered and how they could best be used to benefit their tribe. They knew how to read the cycles of nature that told them when to plant and harvest their crops. They knew the animals that lived in their region and they knew how to hunt successfully for them. They knew where they could find tasty wild fruits and berries to supplement their diet. And they knew which plants could be used as effective medicines to fight disease. This closeness with nature and knowledge of the land's natural resources is one reason why Native Americans were so reluctant to leave their homes for reservations in unfamiliar territory.

Native Americans had a great reverence for the environment and did as little to damage it as possible. Most tribes were careful not to take more out of the environment than they needed to live comfortably. They realized that if they hunted too much game, there might not be enough for next season. For the same reason, they were careful not to cut too many trees, overfish their streams, or eat so much corn that there would not be enough seed left to plant next spring's crop.

These beliefs were nearly the opposite of those held by the European settlers. Most Europeans believed that individuals, as well as nations, should own and develop property. Europeans had lived under crowded conditions at home, and they thought it was wasteful not to get the most use and profit out of a piece of land.

Consequentially, European settlers saw the land that Native Americans had kept in its natural state as wild and undeveloped. They felt that if land was not being farmed by European settlers, built on, or otherwise developed, it was literally going to waste.

For that reason and many more, white settlers concluded that if these "savages" were not making full use of their land, they did not really own it or need it. They felt that it was their right to take it away from them. John Winthrop, a Puritan English lawyer who became governor of the Massachusetts Bay colony in 1630, declared that the bulk of the land in America was *vacuum domicilium*, legally wasteland because the Native Americans had not "subdued" it by farming the land or building on it.[9]

These opposing beliefs concerning land ownership and use were among the most important elements of the conflict that eventually led to whites forcing Native Americans off of their ancestral homeland and onto reservations controlled by the United States government.

The European settlers' attitude toward America's native populations prevailed for many years. Nearly three centuries after the first European colonies had been established in North America, much of the nation's white population remained convinced that the Native Americans' right to live where they wanted was not nearly as important as the progress they saw in the spread of their own civilization across the continent.

The Handbook of American Indians, published by the Smithsonian Institution's Bureau of American Ethnology in 1910, illustrates this view. The handbook justified the United States government's policy of forcing Native Americans to live on reservations by saying:

> A natural result of land cessions by the Indians to the U.S. Government was the establishment of reservations for the natives. This was necessary not only in order to provide them with homes and land for cultivation, but to avoid disputes in regard to boundaries and to bring them more easily under control of the Government by confining them to given limits. . . . It may be attributed primarily to the increase of the white population and the consequent necessity of confining the aboriginal [native] population to narrower limits.[10]

With whites in possession of most of their former territory, the struggle of America's native population was not only to hold onto what they had left of their land. It was also, in the face of the nation's dominant white European culture, to hold onto their tribal traditions, religions, and way of life.

EARLY RELATIONS WITH EUROPEAN SETTLERS

During the 1400s and 1500s, the kings and queens of Europe sent explorers all over the world in search of gold, silver, and other valuables. The goal of many of these explorers was to find a shorter path to India. Instead, they found America. Believing they had reached India, they referred to the people that lived in North America as Indians.

Soon the European explorers realized that the land they had reached was not India at all. Instead, it was a different land that no one in Europe knew anything about. To avoid conflicts over the ownership of newly discovered territories in the Americas, a series of agreements were drawn up by European leaders. The Doctrine of Discovery is one of the most important of these agreements. This agreement stated that the right to acquire title to newly discovered land belonged to the nation that funded the expedition.

According to the Doctrine of Discovery, the title to land was only supposed to be transferred at the will of its native owners.[1] But in reality, that provision of the doctrine was seldom honored. Most leaders of European expeditions to the Americas did not really respect the right of non-Christian native peoples to keep their homelands. They saw too much profit in taking it away from them.

The Spanish Discover North America

Spain was the first European nation to establish itself in North America. When the Spanish explorers encountered the natives, they were required by their government to read the following pronouncement to them:

> We ask and require you . . . to acknowledge the Church as ruler and superior of the whole world, and the high priest called the Pope and his name the King [of Spain] as lords of . . . terra firma. . . . [If you submit], we . . . shall receive you in all love and charity, and shall leave you, your wives and children, and your lands, free without servitude. . . . But if you do not [submit] . . . we shall powerfully enter into your country, and shall make war against you. . . . We shall take you, and your wives, and your children, and shall make slaves of them. . . . and we shall take away your goods and shall do you all the harm and damage we can.[2]

The Native Americans, who had never before heard the Spanish language, had no means to comprehend the threat that was being made against them.

The Spanish came up through Mexico and poured into the Pueblo country of southwestern North America in the early 1540s. Their presence was a shock to Native Americans. The Spanish had powerful armies, wore shiny metal suits of armor, and rode on horses—huge beasts that the natives had never seen before. The Spanish possessed weapons that were far more deadly than anything the native population had ever encountered. Spanish soldiers routinely killed anyone who resisted their advances as they plundered the Native American cities and towns in search of gold, silver, precious jewels, and other valuable items.

The Spanish expeditions moved through the southwestern region of what would become the United States in search of gold and silver. But the stockpiles of precious metals they hoped to find did not exist. The Spanish then decided to start mining and agricultural enterprises in North America. They claimed the Native American land they wanted in the name of Spain, and used the tribes they conquered as slave laborers to work the plantations.

English Relations With the Natives

English settlers arrived on North America's East Coast in the early 1600s. Some came, as the Spanish did, to explore the land for riches. But many more English settlers came to North America to make a new home for themselves.

These people had chosen to leave their homes in England and come to America for a wide variety of reasons. Some left England to escape religious persecution. Other English colonists came with dreams of making more profit in the New World than they could in England. To many, leaving England and sailing to America was their only hope of having a piece of land of their own.

The first group of English settlers to set up a successful colony in North America arrived in 1607. Their ship, carrying 104 colonists, landed at what would become known as Jamestown, Virginia. Many of the Jamestown settlers were professional soldiers, sons of British noblemen, and their servants.

At first, the Native Americans that lived in the area were wary of the settlers' intentions. The tribes, which were under the leadership of Chief Powhatan (also called Wahunsonacook), were already having problems with aggressive tribes that lived to the west. For protection, they had formed an alliance with nearly thirty other coastal tribes, consisting of approximately twenty thousand members, to ward off possible attacks.

So while Chief Powhatan saw the settlers as a possible threat, he also saw the white European newcomers, with their huge ships and powerful firearms, as potential allies against his tribe's enemies.

The European settlers knew that they were at a disadvantage. They were not at all familiar with their new home. While they had more advanced weapons than the Native Americans, they did not have sufficient military force to protect themselves from an extended attack. So it was vital to the survival of the settlement for the colonists to form a friendly alliance with their Native American neighbors.

To obtain Chief Powhatan's friendship and ensure peace, the colony's leader, Captain John Smith, brought gifts to the tribe. He gave their chief a golden crown and declared him to be "King Powhatan." In return for these gestures of friendship, the tribe offered the colonists food and taught the settlers how to raise their own food the following spring. Because of their assistance, the Jamestown settlement flourished.

Captain John Smith, the leader of the Jamestown settlement, said of the tribe's hospitality:

> It pleased God . . . to move the Indians to bring us Corne, ere it was halfe ripe, to refresh us, when we rather expected when they would destroy us . . . the Indians brought us great store bothe of Corne and bread already made: and also there came such abundance of Fowles into the Rivers, as greatly refreshed our weake estates . . . With fish, oysters, bread, and deere, they kindly traded with me and my men, beeing no lesse in doubt of my intent, then I of theirs.[3]

In 1620, when another group of English settlers landed at what would later be known as Plymouth, Massachusetts, they were in much the same situation as the Jamestown settlers. They did not have sufficient supplies for the winter, and most of the colonists were not accustomed to providing for themselves from the resources the land offered.

Samoset, from the Pemaquid tribe, and Massasoit, Squanto, and Hobomah, from the Wampanoag tribe, were the first Native Americans to meet the Pilgrims. They all knew some English, which they had learned from explorers who had stopped there years earlier. They took pity on the ill-prepared colonists and offered them food. Later, they showed the colonists how to plant and cultivate corn and other vegetables.

The leader of the Plymouth colony, William Bradford, said of Squanto:

> Squanto continued with them, and was their interpreter, and was a spetiall instrument sent of God for their good beyond their expectation. He directed them how to set their corne, wher to take fish, and to procure other comodities, and was also their pilott to bring them to unknowne places for their profitt, and never left them till he dyed.[4]

In the early years of colonization, keeping peace with nearby tribes of Native Americans was vital to the colony's survival. Even though the European settlers had more powerful weapons than the Native Americans had, they were vastly outnumbered. European settlements were often surrounded on all sides by powerful tribes who could easily overcome them.

While there were occasional outbreaks of hostility between the two peoples, relations between the early European settlers and the Native Americans were generally peaceful. Both sides had items that the other wanted to trade for. The European settlers needed food, animal skins, and furs, while the Native Americans wanted metal tools, weapons, cooking utensils, and other items that were available only from the colonists.

The Native Americans taught Europeans how to raise corn, potatoes, squash, pumpkins, tobacco, tomatoes, and many other crops that were unknown in Europe. The Europeans, in exchange, introduced Native Americans to wheat, oats, barley, rice, grapes, and melons.

During those early years of white settlement, there were so few Europeans in North America that land ownership had not yet become a serious issue. As long as the European colonists treated the Native Americans in a friendly manner, most of the tribes they encountered were willing to coexist with them. The natives opened their hearts and shared their food, land, and resources with these strange new people who had come from across the ocean.

Religious Intolerance

But once the colonies became self-sufficient, peaceful relations with the Native Americans often deteriorated. The kindness the tribes had shown the colonists was quickly forgotten. The fact that Native Americans did not live in the manner that Europeans thought of as civilized caused many white settlers to look down on them.

The European colonists came from a world where nearly everyone believed in some form of Christianity. Because of this, many European settlers had little, if any, tolerance for Native Americans who refused to abandon their religious beliefs in favor of Christianity. Although many of the settlers were fleeing from the intolerance they had experienced in Europe, they were insistent on imposing their beliefs on the Native Americans. Instead of readily accepting Christianity, the vast majority of Native Americans preferred to worship in the traditional ways of their ancestors. Even the Native Americans who did accept Christianity during this period usually practiced it along with their own Native spiritual practices. This was totally unacceptable to the European missionaries.

The European settlers' intolerance of Native American lifestyles and beliefs, along with the colonists' growing need for land, made the new European arrivals feel justified in forcing them off their ancestral territory in 1620, William Bradford, the leader of the Plymouth colony, wrote of:

> Those vast & unpeopled countries of America, which are frutfull & fitt for habitation, being devoyd of all civill inhabitants, wher ther are only savage & brutish men, which range up and downe.[5]

At this point, many early European settlers viewed the Native Americans as nothing but a nuisance that had to be dealt with until the white settlements became strong enough to push them out of their way. This attitude would eventually result in Native Americans being forced off their homelands and onto government-controlled reservations.

Chapter 3

AS THE COLONIES GREW

As the colonies in North America grew, news about their success spread rapidly through- out Europe. It was indeed possible for European settlements to thrive in this land across the Atlantic Ocean. North America was a vast land of boundless resources. In comparison to the limited land resources in Europe, endless acres of land were available to be farmed in America. There were new foods, such as corn and squash, that very few Europeans had ever tasted. There were lush pine forests brimming with animals that colonists hunted for meat, fur, and skins. The only problem was that the land of North America, which was being praised throughout Europe for its unlimited bounty and opportunity, was already inhabited.

The mass migration of Europeans to North America gave hope to many thousands of people who wanted to escape the problems of Europe and start over. But this spread of the European population into North America and the economic development that followed had disastrous consequences for Native Americans. The rapid expansion of European colonies along North America's eastern seaboard led to an unending demand that Native Americans give up more and more of their land for white settlements.

Until the Europeans had firmly established themselves in North America, many Native Americans did not fully realize that their land, their way of life, and their very existence were in danger of being destroyed.

European Diseases Plague Native Americans

During this time, European diseases were rapidly spreading throughout the continent. After contact with white settlers, Native Americans suddenly became ill and died in large numbers. Smallpox, measles, whooping cough, tuberculosis, and other European diseases all caused severe epidemics among the Native Americans. These diseases, for which the Native Americans had no immunity, seriously weakened the strength of the tribes they struck. In many cases, more than 50 percent of a tribe's population died of an epidemic. Some tribes, including the Patuxet tribe in New England, were completely wiped out by European diseases.

These epidemics gave European colonists a military advantage by weakening the Native Americans' ability to defend their land. This made it possible for white settlers to seize territory from the tribes they had once feared.

Some colonists even went as far as believing that the devastating effect of European diseases on Native Americans was a sign of God's approval of their efforts to claim the land. In 1634, the first governor of the Massachusetts colony wrote: "For the natives, they are nearly all dead of the smallpox, so as the Lord hath cleared our title to what we possess."[1]

Wave after wave of European diseases swept through the continent. Even Native Americans that had never seen a white settler became ill. They caught European illnesses because they made contact with tribes who had dealt with the settlers.

The plague of European diseases had an additional effect on some tribes. It made them even more determined to drive the white settlers out of their land.

The Pequot Tribe of New England

One of the most powerful tribes in New England, the Pequot, soon grew tired of dealing with the white newcomers. They were tired of suffering with their diseases and their demands.[2] In 1634, some of the tribe's warriors attacked English trading ships that were anchored along New England's shores. The Pequot killed nine English traders and plundered their goods. As a result of this attack, the Massachusetts Bay General Court demanded that the leaders of the Pequot tribe take responsibility for the attack. As part of the fine, the leaders were forced to turn over a large area of tribal land in present-day Connecticut to the colonists.

But this did not put an end to the Pequot raiding. In the following years, Pequot warriors attacked isolated English settlements in the region, killing approximately thirty colonists. They also took women and children into captivity. In May 1636, the Massachusetts Bay General Court declared war on the Pequot tribe.

With the assistance of Narragansett and Wampanoag warriors, Captain John Mason led colonial soldiers into Pequot territory. They burned villages throughout the region. Just before the war ended in 1637, the colonial solders set the main Pequot village, near present-day Mystic, Connecticut, on fire, killing nearly five hundred Pequot men, women, and children. After the Pequot were conquered, much of southern New England was opened for white settlements.

Puritans Make Demands on the Tribes

With their most powerful enemy out of the way, many colonial leaders grew bolder in the demands they made on the remaining tribes. Puritan leaders demanded that nearby tribes honor not only the English colonial laws, but their religious rules as well. When Native Americans committed offenses such as not keeping the Sabbath, Puritan leaders in New England felt justified in seizing tribal lands as punishment.

Eventually, the Puritans decided that the best way to convert the Native Americans to Christianity was to isolate them from the influence of other tribes.[3] So the Puritans began to relocate small tribes that were too small or weak to defend themselves on plots of land known as reservations.

Early Reservations

In 1638, Puritan colonial authorities created the first official reservation for Native Americans. A twelve hundred-acre reservation was set up at present-day New Haven, Connecticut, for the forty-seven surviving members of the Quinnipiac tribe.

The Puritan leaders promised to protect the Quinnipiac from hostile tribes that lived nearby. But in return, they established strict rules that they expected the Quinnipiac to follow. The Quinnipiac were forbidden to leave the reservation without permission, and they were not permitted to receive visits from Native Americans of other tribes. Reservation rules also forbade the sale of liquor, guns, and ammunition to the Quinnipiac people. The Puritans referred to Native Americans that lived at the New Haven reservation as "praying Indians."

But the Puritans' motives for keeping the Quinnipiac confined on a reservation was not entirely religious. While Puritan missionaries were teaching the Quinnipiac to accept their religion and way of life, colonial leaders were dividing the natives' homelands into farms for British settlers.[4]

The idea of establishing reservations proved to be popular with colonial leaders throughout New England. Once a tribe of Native Americans was placed on a reservation, it was relatively easy to control them and to take over their land. In 1651, the Massachusetts General Court set up an eight-thousand-acre reservation for the Natick tribe. Once a Natick had proved to the reservation's white overseers that he could live "civilly and orderly," a parcel of land was deeded to him for farming and raising livestock. Carpenters from the Puritan colony were sent in to help the Natick build European-style homes on their land. This reservation was the first to allot individual parcels of land to Native American families.

In the following years, several additional reservations were established in New England in an effort to civilize and convert Native Americans. One such reservation was set up in southeastern Connecticut for Pequot tribe members who had survived the war.

In 1656, the Massachusetts General Court appointed Daniel Gookin as the first Superintendent of Indian Affairs. He was put in charge of the Puritan efforts to civilize the tribes.

The colonial officials appointed a Native American as governor of each tribe. He, along with an English supervisor, was put in charge of the reservation. Every tribe that had been placed on a reservation was required to pay an annual tax or tribute to the colonial government.

The Puritans decided that the reservations they set up should be operated under an English legal system. A court system based on English law was established so that tribal members accused of a crime could be tried. Eventually, Native Americans were allowed to have their testimony heard in court and to serve as jurors. Through the establishment of reservations and other missionary efforts, the Puritans converted nearly 20 percent of Native Americans living in New England to Christianity by 1670.

Backlash Against European Rule

Despite their apparent progress, the Puritans' efforts to civilize Native Americans was not working as well as they had hoped. Both on and off the reservations, growing numbers of Native Americans were becoming weary of the new rules they were forced to live by. Even Native Americans that the Puritans believed they had converted longed for the life they had had before the colonists came. Certainly there were advantages to the farm tools, livestock, and other modern conveniences that the European colonists brought to North America. But to many Native Americans, they were not worth giving up their land and traditional culture.

King Philip, chief of the Wampanoag tribe, was the leader of the Native American resistance against the Puritans. He rallied nearby tribes, including the Nipmucks and the Narragansetts to attack white settlements in southern New England in 1675 and 1676. In May 1676, the colonial armies killed King Philip and defeated the last of his warriors.

The tribes that fought against the settlers were forced to give up most of western Massachusetts to the white colonists as war retribution. The Puritans also took many members of these tribes into captivity and sold them as slaves.

The attacks on white settlements during King Philip's War solidified the Puritans' feelings against the Native Americans. Puritan minister Cotton Mather told his congregation that Native Americans were "the accursed seed of Canaan" and it was "the duty of good Christians to exterminate them."[5] It was during this period that the Massachusetts General Court decided to strip Native Americans of even larger tracts of land as they crowded the tribes onto increasingly smaller reservations.

As the European settlements took up more of their land, Native Americans were often driven back into the territory of unfriendly tribes. This caused an increase in wars between tribes that in the past had been able to avoid each other.

But regardless of the difficulties their presence was causing Native Americans, Europeans were in North America to stay. Each ship full of settlers that arrived in North America meant that more land would be needed for whites to settle and farm. And that land would come from the estate of Native Americans.

Chapter 4

NATIVE AMERICAN INVOLVEMENT IN WHITE WARS

As the Europeans continued to colonize America, the Native Americans soon learned that settlers coming from different nations had many quarrels with each other. Some disagreements had to do with trade policy or government affairs in Europe. Others had to do with territorial borders in North America. Still others had to do with disagreements between various religious groups. But those quarrels that concerned Native Americans the most had to do with who held the balance of military power in North America. The group that held this power would determine the fate of the Native American people and what remained of their land.

The French and Indian War

The French and Indian War was the first major war between white powers to involve Native American tribes. This war, which was fought between 1754 and 1763, started when colonists from France and England clashed over the settlement of land to the west of the Appalachian Mountains.

The Iroquois Confederation, a group of Native American tribes that lived in what is now central New York State, sided with the British colonies. This was partly because the British provided them with valuable trade goods. The tribes living in the Ohio territory sided with the French, who paid good prices for their furs, furnished them with guns and ammunition, and promised to protect Native American land against the expansion of British colonies.

Both groups of Europeans encouraged the tribes that sided with them to launch attacks against their enemy's settlements. They also encouraged them to fight the tribes that sided with their adversary.

When the French and Indian War ended in 1763, France was forced to turn over all of its land claims west of the Appalachian Mountains to Britain. This was a serious blow to the security of the Native Americans that lived there. The French who had lived among the Native Americans there were mostly trappers and traders. But the British, the Native Americans knew, were always hungry to obtain more land for their farms and settlements. With their former French allies gone, Native American tribes to the west of the Appalachian Mountains feared that British forces from the East would attempt to drive them out of the territory.[1]

To deal with this threat to their land, many of the tribes that lived in the region organized under Ottawa Chief Pontiac to defend their land. In 1763, they staged an uprising against the white settlers that had illegally moved onto land west of the Appalachian Mountains. During the uprising, the Native Americans captured nine British forts and killed approximately one thousand white settlers.

The British called this uprising "Pontiac's Conspiracy." They retaliated by sending in troops to force back the Native Americans and burn their villages. They also tried to weaken the military strength of the tribes by delivering blankets from a smallpox hospital to the tribes to infect the natives. But even with a smallpox epidemic raging through the area, the Native

American tribes proved to be too formidable a foe for the British to defeat.

In the fall of that year, the British decided that it would be in their best interest to try to put an end to the fighting by negotiating a peace treaty with the Native Americans. As a part of this treaty, the British government forbade their citizens to settle on Native American territory west of the Appalachian Mountains. The Royal Proclamation Concerning America, issued on October 7, 1763, by the British government, stated:

> Several nations or tribes of Indians, with whom we are connected, and who live under our protection, should not be molested or disturbed in the possession of such parts of our dominions and territories as, not having been ceded to, or purchased by us, are reserved to them, or any of them, as their hunting grounds . . . And we do further declair . . . to reserve under our sovereignty, protection, and dominion, for the use of the said Indians, all the land and territories not included within the limits of our [governments].[2]

But despite this treaty, white settlers did not stay off the land the British government had reserved for the Native Americans. Colonial governments, as well as individual white settlers, ignored the treaty and invaded territories that clearly belonged to the tribes. To keep peace with the Native Americans, the British government sent soldiers to keep colonists from crossing into Native American territory. The British government taxed the colonists to pay for stationing these additional soldiers. Eventually the closing of the western frontier to white settlement, as well as the additional taxes imposed by the British government to enforce the treaty they made with the Native Americans, led many white American colonists to push for independence from Britain.

The Revolutionary War

The Revolutionary War, which started in 1775, was the next major white conflict to involve Native Americans. In exchange for Native American support, the British government pledged to defend the Native Americans' right to retain ownership of land that white settlers, under America's colonial government, had illegally occupied. British officials assured the Native Americans that if they fought with the British and helped them to stay in power, they would make the white settlers stop their westward expansion. They promised to make settlers stay off land that was still occupied by Native Americans, and to force white settlers who were already trespassing there to leave. As a result, most Native American tribes in the region sided with the British.

The British government also gained the friendship of the Native Americans by providing them with valuable trade goods, such as guns, powder, lead flints, cooking utensils, cloth, and other useful items. These goods were preferred by most tribes to those produced by the American colonists because they were of better quality and were less expensive.

The colonial government of the United States, on the other hand, had little to offer the Native American tribes. White settlers had routinely taken Native American land without permission, and the colonial government itself had repeatedly bullied tribal leaders into selling or giving away land they wished to keep. As a result, few tribes wished to support the colonies in their fight against the British.

The colonial government soon realized that the best they could hope for from Native American tribes was neutrality. A congressional address to the Six Nations of the Iroquois Confederation on July 13, 1775, said:

> This is a family quarrel between us and Old England. You Indians are not concerned in it. We don't wish you to take

up the hatchet against the king's troops. We desire you to remain at home, and not join on either side, but keep the hatchet buried deep.[3]

Less than a year later, in May of 1776, the colonial government decided to actively attempt to recruit Native Americans to fight on their side of the conflict. But during the entire Revolutionary War, the colonial government was able to obtain the assistance of only a few tribes. Even so, the colonial government was able to win victory over the British troops and their Native American allies and hold the balance of power along the nation's eastern seaboard.

The New Nation's Native American Policy

In 1783, the Treaty of Paris officially marked the end of the Revolutionary War. As a part of the agreement, England signed over the Northwest Territory, which was north of the Ohio River and west of Pittsburgh, to the United States. Many of the tribes that lived in the Northwest Territory had sided with England during the war. Because they fought against the United States, most American government officials felt that these tribes had waged "unprovoked war" on the country, and thereby forfeited the title to their land.[4]

To deal with the tribes more effectively, the new United States government wanted to create a single, coordinated policy for dealing with the Native Americans. Up to that time, the individual states and territories had often acted independently in dealing with nearby tribes. The Articles of the Confederation, which were written as guidelines for the United States central government, stated that Congress "has the sole and exclusive right and power of . . . regulating trade and managing all affairs with Indians, not members of any states, provided that the legislative right of any state within its own limits be not infringed or violated."[5]

Unlike some government leaders of the time, President George Washington had no desire to use unnecessary military force against the Native Americans. He hoped that "an orderly expansion [by white settlers] would compel the Indians to retire [leave the area]."[6] However, he did want the tribes to become civilized in the ways of white society and to give up lands to the United States government as they were needed for colonial expansion.

There already was a tremendous demand for more land to be opened for white settlement. Almost as soon as the Revolutionary War was over, white settlers started to pour across the Appalachian Mountains and into Native American lands north and west of the Ohio River. Many of the soldiers who fought on the side of the continental government in the Revolutionary War had been promised tracts of land as pay, and were anxious to claim it. Other settlers merely took advantage of the lack of government enforcement, and claimed Native American land illegally. They became known as squatters—people who moved onto a piece of land without paying for it. This scramble for land resulted in thousands of white settlers crossing into what was still legally Native American land. In doing this, they willfully ignored agreements that had been made in good faith with tribal leaders.

All of this angered Native American leaders. To prevent outbreaks of hostilities, Congress issued a proclamation in 1783 that prohibited white settlement or purchase of Native American lands that were outside of state jurisdiction. But despite the proclamation, white settlers continued to cross the Ohio River and trespass onto lands that still belonged to the Natives.

In 1787, Congress decided to devise a plan for a more orderly development of the northwestern territory—present-day Ohio, Indiana, Illinois, Michigan, and Wisconsin. The result of this decision, the Northwest Ordinance, stated in part:

The utmost good faith shall always be observed towards the Indians; their lands and property shall never be taken without their consent; and in their property, rights, and liberty, they shall never be invaded or disturbed, unless in just and lawful wars authorized by Congress; but laws founded in justice and humility shall from time to time be made for preventing wrongs being done to them, and for preserving peace and friendship with them.[7]

In reality, the provisions of the Northwest Ordinance concerning the rights of Native Americans were not honored by the United States government. Instead, the ordinance was misused to invoke congressional power against the tribes, in violation of both the letter and the spirit of the law. It gave the United States government a means to extinguish Native American land title (ownership), divide the land into tracts, and sell it to white settlers.

The Native American tribes did not give up their land without a fight. Little Turtle, a chief of the Miami tribe who lived near what is now Fort Wayne, Indiana, formed an alliance with nearby tribes to push the white settlers out of their territory. Between 1783 and 1790, their warriors killed approximately fifteen hundred white settlers.[8]

When President George Washington heard about the attacks, he did not hesitate to send in troops to attempt to force out the tribes that had raided the northwestern settlements. The first military expedition, which was sent into the area in 1790, was badly defeated and driven back.

The next year, Washington sent in troops under General Arthur St. Clair, Indian superintendent and governor of the Northwest Territory, to attempt to put an end to the hostilities. The Native American alliance dealt St. Clair's troops a surprising defeat. In that battle, which took place about one hundred miles north of present-day Cincinnati, Ohio, the Native alliance killed nearly nine hundred colonial soldiers.

But this was only a temporary victory for the Native Americans. In the fall of 1793, the United States government sent three thousand more troops into the area under Major General Anthony Wayne. Wayne's troops defeated the Native American alliance, then went on to destroy every Native American village they could find.

The next spring, Wayne called together the leaders of the Native American tribes that had been involved in the war and compelled them to sign a treaty to surrender nearly all of present-day Ohio and the southeastern part of Indiana to the United States government. This became known as the Treaty of Greenville. In return, the United States government allowed the tribes to live on a reserve, which would be located on their tribal homelands. The government also promised to deliver the tribes twenty thousand dollars worth of goods and to make a payment of ten thousand dollars each year, to be divided among the tribes that signed the treaty.

But the struggle for Native Americans to hold onto their land was far from over. Even after this bitter defeat, Native Americans in other parts of the country had begun to form new alliances among the tribes to fight against the spread of white settlers into their territory.

Tecumseh and the War of 1812

Tecumseh, a Shawnee chief, and his brother Tenshwataw, known as "The Prophet," were among the most important leaders in this movement. Tecumseh traveled from the Great Lakes to the Gulf of Mexico to gain support for their movement. He spoke to tribes and tried to convince them to unite and save their land. Tecumseh said in a speech in 1812:

> Every year our white intruders become more greedy, exacting, oppressive and overbearing. . . . Wants and oppressions are our lot. . . . Are we not being stripped day by day of the little that remains of our ancient liberty? . . .

Unless every tribe unanimously combines to give a check to the ambition and avarice of the whites, they will soon conquer us apart and disunited, and we will be driven away from our native country and scattered as autumnal leaves before the wind.[9]

The War of 1812, between America and England, gave Native Americans new opportunities to try to protect what was left of their land. Tecumseh took his plea for help to the British military leaders, who were waging war against the United States government. They led him to believe that if he sided with them in the War of 1812 (also known as the Second Revolutionary War), they would help him to drive the white settlers out of Native American land.

Tecumseh continued to travel and speak to tribal leaders and warriors everywhere about the necessity of moving against the United States government as soon as possible. He wanted to form alliances among the tribes to fight the Americans. Tecumseh said, "Here is a chance . . . such as will never occur again—for us Indians of North America to form ourselves into one great combination."[10]

Tecumseh gathered a large war party and marched to join the British. At one time during the struggle, Tecumseh commanded nearly three thousand Native American warriors from over thirty tribes. Tecumseh fought valiantly with the British in the War of 1812 to protect his land, until he was killed in the Battle of Thames on October 5, 1813, in Ontario, Canada.

When the United States defeated Britain in the War of 1812, the tribes that had fought as allies of Britain were left in an unenviable position. Deprived of military assistance from their former British allies, the tribes' power was so weak that the United States government was able to force their chiefs to sign a series of treaties requiring the natives to give up ownership of large areas of land.

The Redsticks and General Jackson

In the Southeast, another battle over control of Native American land was brewing. A pro-war division of the Creeks known as the Redsticks decided to reject everything that had to do with white civilization and live in the traditional ways of their ancestors. Part of the Redsticks' task in disassociating themselves with white society was to force white settlers and armies to leave Creek land.

The hostilities started in 1813 when the Redsticks massacred 107 soldiers, 160 civilians, and 100 slaves at Fort Mims, a military post on the lower Alabama River. General Andrew Jackson, who was later to become president, retaliated by waging a campaign to destroy every town he could find in the upper part of Creek territory. He ordered his soldiers to burn entire villages. They killed men, women, and children and destroyed the Creek's crops and possessions. General Jackson later gained fame for leading the troops that defeated the Redsticks on March 27, 1814, at Horseshoe Bend, Alabama. In one battle, Jackson and his five-thousand-man militia killed eight hundred Creeks, with few casualties on Jackson's side.

General Jackson held the entire Creek nation responsible for the actions of the Redsticks. In August 1814, Jackson called the Creek chiefs together to lay out his terms of peace. Jackson forced the Creeks to sign treaties giving up nearly 22 million acres of land in Georgia and Alabama. This was nearly two thirds of the Creek nation. Under the dictates of the treaty, many bands of Creeks that had not fought against the United States were also forced to give up large sections of their ancestral homelands. When Big Warrior, a leader of a friendly Creek tribe that had not fought against the United States protested to Jackson against the government taking their land, Jackson angrily snapped back:

Listen . . . The United States would have been justified by the Great Spirit, had they taken all the land of the nation; . . . Listen—the truth is, the great body of the Creek chiefs and warriors did not respect the power of the United States—They thought we were an insignificant nation— that we would be overpowered by the British.[11]

White settlers were anxious to use this newly opened land in the South to grow cotton, tobacco, and other profitable crops. Soon, even more land was demanded from the tribes. In the ten years following the defeat of the Redsticks, the United States government pressured Native American leaders to sign a series of treaties turning over control of three fourths of Florida and Alabama, and large portions of what are now Mississippi, Georgia, Kentucky, and North Carolina.

There never seemed to be enough land to satisfy the ever-growing demand of white settlers. No matter how much land Native American leaders were forced to sign away, the United States government always wanted to take even more from them.

5 Chapter

NATIVE AMERICAN REMOVAL POLICY

It did not take long for white settlers to occupy most of the arable land along America's East Coast. By the late 1700s, more than 3.9 million white settlers were already living in the United States. Most lived within fifty miles of the Atlantic Ocean. North America's non-native population was rapidly expanding beyond the size that existing white settlements could support. This resulted in white settlers demanding that the government make more Native American land available for their farms and settlements.

By the early 1800s, many United States government leaders felt that the best way to make room for more white settlements was to relocate the eastern tribes of Native Americans to the west of the Mississippi River. At the time, most white Americans thought of the vast grassy plains that lay west of the Mississippi River as the Great American Desert. Few white people lived there, and those who had visited the region brought back reports of endless grasslands that were not suitable for European agricultural methods.

Jefferson's Policy

President Thomas Jefferson was one of the first national leaders to suggest relocating Native Americans west of the Mississippi River. At the time Jefferson took office in 1800, white settlements were rapidly expanding beyond the eastern seaboard colonies. Seven hundred thousand white settlers were already living west of the Appalachian Mountains, a mountain chain that runs from Quebec to Alabama. In some parts of this region, white settlers already outnumbered Native Americans eight to one. Many of these settlers were trespassing on Native American land without the permission of the United States or tribal governments. The belief that the white settlers' need for land was more important than that of the Native Americans was widespread.[1]

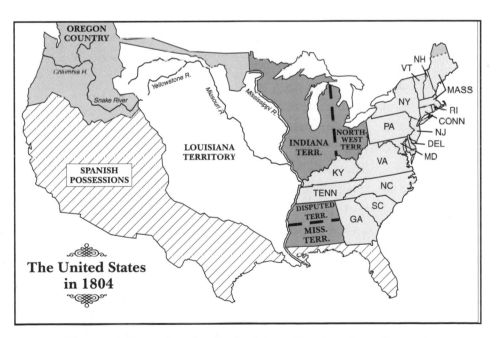

Thomas Jefferson bought the Louisiana Territory from France in 1803. He hoped to relocate the Native Americans to the area west of the Mississippi River..

Because of this uncontrollable expansion of white settlements, Thomas Jefferson felt that relocating Native American tribes west of the Mississippi River was the best answer to the "Indian issue." It would make more land available to white settlers, while at the same time it would give missionaries and educators a chance to "civilize" Native Americans and gradually incorporate them into white society. Jefferson felt that civilizing the Native Americans and teaching them to live as the Europeans did was the only way to ensure their survival. In 1803, President Jefferson said:

> I consider the business of hunting has already become insufficient to furnish clothing and subsistence to the Indians. The promotion of agriculture, therefore, and household manufacture, are essential to their preservation. . . . This will enable them to live on much smaller portions of land, our increasing numbers will be calling for more land, and thus a coincidence of interest.[2]

But unlike some government leaders of the time, Thomas Jefferson did not want to remove the Native American tribes by force. He hoped to work out an agreement that would satisfy both sides of the issue.

When Thomas Jefferson was in office as president, he made three attempts to voluntarily remove tribes living in the southeastern states to portions of the Louisiana Territory, which the United States had recently purchased from France. Part of his reason for acquiring the Louisiana Territory was to make a home for the eastern tribes that were being crowded out of their territory by white settlers. But the Native American leaders, who from past experiences had come to distrust promises made by America's white government, refused to uproot their people and move the tribe to a land they did not know.

While Jefferson was negotiating voluntary removal with tribal leaders, other United States government officials were already hard at work pressuring Native Americans to sign away their land. William Henry Harrison, the governor of the Indiana Territory and future president of the United States, was a shrewd negotiator for the government. He obtained land from the Delaware, Ottawa, Kickapoo, and other tribes.

Between 1800 and 1809, Harrison was responsible for negotiating fifteen treaties with the Native Americans. These treaties gave the nation's white government control over much of Indiana and Illinois, as well as portions of what are now Ohio, Michigan, and Wisconsin. The payment Native Americans received for this land was less than a penny an acre.

In one treaty signed at Fort Wayne in 1809, Harrison persuaded the Delaware and Potawatomi tribes to sign over 3 million acres of land in Indiana to the United States government for $7,000 and an annual payment of $1,750. The tribes then lived on a tiny portion of their former homeland.[3]

Presidents James Monroe and John Adams followed Jefferson's example of asking, but not forcing, Native Americans to relocate to the West. But few tribes wished to move, and the issue did not go away.

By the late 1820s, the United States government had gained sufficient military power that they could conceivably force any tribe living to the east of the Mississippi River off their land. And that is exactly what many white Americans wanted them to do.

Jackson Forces Tribes to Relocate

Andrew Jackson, who became president in 1829, took the most militant stand yet against Native Americans. Jackson was well known throughout the country as a frontiersman and an "Indian fighter" who had won many battles for the United States during the Revolutionary War.

Jackson was staunch in his support of the continued expansion of white settlements into Native American land, and was willing to take any measures necessary to move Native American tribes out of the path of white America's progress. By the time of his election, the white population of the United States had swelled to nearly 13 million, and more land was needed to accommodate their needs.

President Jackson was quick to put his ideas into action. In 1830, he introduced the Indian Removal Bill, which made it possible to legally force all tribes remaining in the East to relocate to Indian Territory, an area west of the Mississippi River that was made up of the future states of Iowa, Kansas, Oklahoma, and Arkansas. Those who sided with Jackson claimed that removal was being proposed in the best interest of the Native Americans. Without being banished from the path of white civilization, supporters of the bill claimed, Native Americans would not be able to survive at all.

But not all lawmakers saw it that way. Several liberal senators and congressmen from New England believed that Native Americans should not be forced to move against their will. One opponent of the bill, Representative Edward Everett of Massachusetts, said:

> Whoever read of such a project? Ten or fifteen thousand families, to be rooted up, and carried a hundred, aye, a thousand miles into the wilderness! There is not such a thing in the annals of mankind. . . . To remove them against their will, by thousands, to a distant and different country, where they must lead a new life, and form other habits, and encounter the perils and hardships of a wilderness . . . They are not barbarians; they are essentially civilized people. . . . They are planters and farmers, they are tradespeople and mechanics, they have cornfields and orchards, looms and workshops, schools and churches, and orderly institutions![4]

The bill was hotly debated, but passed through Congress by a 102 to 97 margin. The Indian Removal Bill was the first step towards the creation of a national reservation system. It was designed to force Native Americans off their ancestral homelands and into specific areas where the government could eventually control their movement, economy, lifestyle, and even their religious practices.

The Removal of Eastern Tribes

Once the Indian Removal Bill was passed, Jackson's first priority was to persuade Native American tribes living in Alabama and Mississippi to relocate to Indian Territory. Jackson wanted to make it clear to the tribal leaders that the only way they could have peaceful relations with the United States government was to relocate to the Indian Territory. Jackson sent an army major to the Choctaw and Cherokee chiefs with these instructions:

> Say to the chiefs and warriors that I am their friend, that I wish to act as their friend but they must, by removing from the limits of the States of Mississippi and Alabama and by being settled on the lands I offer them, put it in my power to be such—There, beyond the limits of any State, in possession of land of their own, which they shall possess as long as Grass grows or water runs. I am and will protect them and be their friend and father.[5]

Andrew Jackson's removal policy was primarily directed against Native Americans that preferred to live in the traditional way, under their own tribal government. He was determined to force them to sign treaties to give up most of their land holdings in Alabama, Georgia, and Mississippi and relocate to Indian Territory.

The Indian Removal Bill did, however, permit members of these tribes to stay in the southeastern states if they agreed to live in the manner of white settlers. In order to stay, they had to take an allotment of land on which to farm, become "civilized," and abide by the laws of the state they lived in.

By this time, many members of the southeastern tribes—the Cherokee, Creek, Chickasaw, Chocktaw, and Seminole—had already made an effort to assimilate in order to survive in the rapidly encroaching white American society. They had set up farms, become American citizens, built churches, and developed a written version of their language in which to communicate on paper. Because of this early effort to assimilate, they are sometimes known as The Five Civilized Tribes.

But when more land was needed for European settlers, the agreements the United States government had made with the Five Civilized Tribes were disregarded. No matter how hard the Native Americans worked to conform to the standards the whites set, the white government still wanted to take their land.

Some tribal leaders went to Washington, D.C., to fight the forced relocation. John Ridge, a Cherokee leader, pleaded for fairness from the United States government as he recounted the changes his people had already made to conform to the wishes of the whites:

> You asked us to throw off the hunter and warrior state:
> We did so—you asked us to form a republican government:
> We did so—adopting your own as a model. You asked us
> to cultivate the earth, and learn the mechanic arts: We did
> so. You asked us to learn to read: We did so. You asked us
> to cast away our idols, and worship your God: We did so.[6]

Although John Ridge did find some support among white lawmakers, it was not enough to stop President Jackson's push for relocation. The Five Civilized Tribes of the Southeast were soon compelled against their will to sign agreements stating that they would move to the Indian Territory in the West.

Government agents that were sent to negotiate treaties with the chiefs were not always honest in their dealings with the

Native Americans. When one group of chiefs refused to sign the treaty, it was taken to another group of leaders from the same tribe whom the agents hoped to pressure in to giving into the government's demands.

One example of this tactic is the Treaty of New Echota, which was signed in 1835 by several Cherokee chiefs after being rejected by Cherokee leader John Ross's group. In the treaty, the government promised to pay the Cherokees $5 million if they would give up 8 million acres of their eastern territory and move west. The government also promised to pay the cost of relocating the tribe, and support them for one year after their arrival. Even though only a small number of the Cherokee chiefs signed the treaty, the government demanded that all bands of the tribe move west.[7]

After the treaties had been signed, some bands of the Five Civilized Tribes decided to start their journey to Indian Territory as soon as possible. They hoped that by doing so, they could obtain the best lands in the area for their people. But other bands were determined to stay on their ancestral homeland until the army forced them to leave.

In 1838, President Martin Van Buren, Jackson's elected successor, lost patience with the bands that refused to leave their homelands. He ordered Major General Winfield Scott to use whatever force was necessary to move the remaining bands of Cherokee into Indian Territory. On May 10 of that year, Major General Winfield Scott told the Cherokee leaders:

> Cherokees! The President of the United States has sent me, with a powerful army, to cause you, in obedience to the Treaty of 1835, to join that part of your people who are already established in prosperity, on the other side of the Mississippi. . . . The full moon of May is already on the wane, and before another shall have passed away, every Cherokee man, woman and child . . . must be in motion to join their brethren in the far West. . . . My troops

already occupy many positions in this country that you are to abandon, and thousands, and thousands are approaching, from every quarter, to render resistance and escape alike hopeless.[8]

In October 1838, the last group of Cherokees began their journey on what became known as the Trail of Tears. Because these bands refused to abandon their land when the government demanded, they did not have time to make preparations for the trip. The soldiers came to move them at gunpoint, and they had no choice but to leave their homes and most of their possessions behind. They took 645 wagons. Some people rode horses, while others walked alongside.

The government gave the job of escorting the Native Americans to Indian Territory to private contractors. Many of these contractors were friends or relatives of high government officials. While some of these contractors were honest, many were corrupt. They kept part of the money that was to be spent feeding and supplying the Native Americans on their long journey. As a result, food and drinking water were in short supply. Many Native Americans became ill and died of sickness, hunger, drought, and exposure. Out of the eighteen thousand Cherokees that were sent out on the infamous Trail of Tears, only about fourteen thousand lived to see the Indian Territory in Oklahoma.

Some bands of Seminoles, led by Chief Osceola, did not allow themselves to be moved to the land the government had reserved for them in Indian Territory. They fought bravely against the white armies that attempted to force them to go there. Kept on the move by American armies, they had to raid white settlements to obtain food when they were hungry. Many escaped into the Florida Everglades, where, on account of the thick vegetation of the huge swamp, it was nearly impossible for the army to track or fight them.

Once they had reached the Everglades, the Seminoles were able to find food in abundance. Both game and fish were plentiful in this swampy area. They built their homes and villages on hammocks—patches of earth above the water level of the swamp. Here, out of the reach of the government troops, they made a new life for their people.

In 1842, the United States government gave up on removing the Seminoles that were living in the Everglades' protection. By that time, the eight-year war against the Seminoles had cost the United States government $20 million and the lives of fifteen hundred troops.

Life in Indian Territory

Many of the Native Americans who survived the march to Indian Territory found that their problems had only begun. Adapting to life on reservations in Indian Territory was a difficult challenge for many from the East. The environment in Indian Territory was in most cases quite different from the lands the tribes had once inhabited. Tribes who had lived for untold generations in the lush pine forests now had to adjust to living on open, nearly treeless regions where many of the plants, animals, and even the cycles of nature were unfamiliar.

Native Americans who were relocated to Indian Territory reservations had other problems as well. While they were trying to find enough food and water to sustain themselves in this new environment, they were forced to deal with local tribes they had never encountered before. They did not know anything about these people or their language, customs, or culture. Native Americans from the Five Civilized Tribes of the East had trouble establishing peaceful relations with the Plains tribes, such as the Comanche, Pawnee, and Kiowa, who lived by hunting buffalo and were always moving from one place to another.

As the government continued to relocate eastern tribes to Indian Territory, the tribes that originally inhabited the area felt increasingly threatened. Buffalo and other game animals were already becoming scarce on the Plains, and numerous fights over hunting rights and land use erupted between the tribes. The newcomers from the East, weakened from their long journey, were in an unfavorable position to defend themselves.

But even during this period of adjustment, United States government officials wanted to relocate even more tribes to the already overcrowded Indian Territory. They felt that by demanding that Native Americans live on smaller and smaller reservations, the government could eventually force the natives to give up hunting entirely and adopt an agricultural way of life. This, government officials believed, was the quickest and cheapest way to compel the Native Americans to leave their traditional "savage" lifestyle behind and become "civilized."[9]

But even Native Americans who decided to cooperate with the government's civilization programs met with much difficulty. The challenges they had to overcome were nearly insurmountable. Many of the tracts of land the tribes were issued in Indian Territory were not suitable for farming, and the agricultural supplies the government sent were rarely adequate. Many tribes could not raise enough food for their members, and had to depend on government rations.

Despite all these problems, the government continued to relocate more tribes to Indian Territory. By the mid-1840s, the majority of Native Americans that once lived east of the Mississippi River had been relocated. In all, the United States government forced at least one hundred thousand Native Americans to leave their ancestral homelands for Indian Territory reservations.

Even before this process of resettlement had been completed, the United States government was looking for more land to open for white settlement. The land the government wanted belonged to the Native American tribes of the West.

Chapter 6

THE WESTERN TRIBES

Before the tribes from the East had adjusted to their new home in Indian Territory, white settlers were pushing into lands to the west of the Mississippi River. The early 1800s had seen white missionaries and explorers from many nations venture into the western parts of North America. Some small, isolated white settlements had even been attempted.

But during the mid-1800s, white settlers found new reasons to push beyond their former boundaries. Cheap land had once again become scarce in the East, and many people were urging the United States government to open more territory for white settlement. Then something happened that forever changed the fate of the western tribes. White explorers discovered gold.

The Gold Rush

The discovery of gold in California in 1848 sent thousands of white settlers and prospectors rushing towards the West. In the first year of the California gold rush, nearly twenty-five thousand whites barreled through Native American land in hopes of finding gold and becoming wealthy. In 1850, California was admitted into statehood, and even more white settlers poured over Native American villages, farms, and hunting grounds. Inevitably, battles over land use broke out between the Native American tribes and the region's new white population.

It soon became apparent to United States government officials that the western tribes would have to be placed on reservations to accommodate the wishes of the prospectors and settlers.

At the time, many of the tribes were still on their original estates. But when Native American villages were in the way of white settler's activities, many of these outsiders thought nothing of destroying them.

Groups of white settlers came together to form "volunteer armies." These armies killed or chased Native Americans away from the areas they wanted to settle. Native American men, women, and children were routinely killed, and sometimes entire Native American villages were destroyed.

Even those Native Americans that did survive the initial attacks on their villages by white settlers were not safe for long. Once Native Americans were forced off their land, many died of starvation, of European diseases, and from attacks by even more white settlers and armies.

California's white government wanted to open Native American land to settlement as quickly as possible. Between 1851 and 1852, they pressured the state's tribes to sign treaties that gave approximately 75 million acres to the United States in exchange for 8.5 million acres of reservation land and a promise of government services and supplies. By 1853, all Native American title to land in California had been extinguished by the white government.

Texas

In the 1850s, white settlers in Texas fought numerous battles with Apaches, Comanches, Kiowas, and other tribes. Some battles were over raids on white settlements and others were over land use. By the mid-1850s, Texas's white government had stripped the state's Native American population of land title and forced them onto two small reservations in the northwestern part of the state.

The Northwestern Tribes

In the early 1850s, the United States government was anxious for white settlers to move into the newly acquired Oregon and Washington territories. In 1850, Congress passed the Oregon Donation Act, giving large grants of land to white settlers who were willing to relocate there. When deposits of gold were discovered throughout the region several years later, white prospectors and settlers poured in to claim their treasures.

The governor of Washington Territory and superintendent of Indian Affairs, Isaac Stevens, was anxious to concentrate the tribes in the Northwest onto reservations so even more land could be opened for white settlement. In 1855, he made a pact with the Blackfoot nation to accept a reduced range in exchange for an annuity of $20,000 for 10 years and $15,000 a year for educating their youth. In another treaty, he obtained nearly 10 million acres of land from the Yakima tribe in the present-day state of Washington, leaving them with a small reservation east of the Cascade Mountains and a promise of government supplies and services.

Only a few of the Yakima chiefs had agreed to the treaty. The other chiefs, who had not been consulted, were angry that the treaty was ratified without their approval. As a result, they went to war against the white settlers. After several victories, the tribes were finally defeated in 1858 in a battle near Spokane, Washington, and were forced to live within the confines of a reservation.[1]

In addition to reducing the Native Americans' land base, these treaties were the beginning of United States government control of the western tribes. It also marked an increase in military surveillance of Native American activities throughout the region. Some tribes struck back against the government, making the 1850s one of the bloodiest decades in the history of the West.

The Civil War Years

The Civil War, which was fought between 1861 and 1865, slowed the pace of forced relocation to Indian Territory. The United States government, as well as the government of the Confederate States of America, which consisted of the eleven southern states that had seceded from the Union, needed nearly every soldier they had available for the war effort. Because of this, fewer troops were available to be sent to fight against the Native Americans.

During the Civil War, the United States government broke even more of the promises they had made to the Native Americans. The government decided that it was more urgent to send food and supplies to soldiers on the battlefield than to send promised supplies to the Native American tribes. Government food deliveries were vital to the survival of many tribes because the reservations were often too small to supply the tribe's needs. In many cases, the soil on reservations was unsuitable for farming and there was not enough game to feed the people.

These broken promises and the lack of food caused some tribes to revolt and attack nearby white settlements. In 1862, for example, the Santee band of Dakotas attacked a white settlement in Minnesota to obtain food and other necessities that the government had denied them.

Southwestern Tribes

By the mid-1850s, many of the tribes that lived in the southwestern region had resorted to raiding settlements of other tribes, as well as those of the whites, to obtain the food and supplies they needed. To help put an end to the problem, the United States government ordered the Union Army to force the Mescalero Apaches and Navajos to relocate to Bosque Redondo, a forty-square-mile reservation in New Mexico.

The natives put up a strong resistance. Only after Kit Carson's troops had stolen their livestock, burned their homes, and destroyed their crops was he able to force bands of Apaches and Navajos to relocate to the Bosque Redondo reservation.

By spring of 1864, nearly eighty-five hundred Apaches and Navajos had been forced to leave their desert homeland and were marched under military guard to the reservation. They were required to stay within the reservation's boundaries and live on government-supplied rations, which were often grossly insufficient for such a large population. The government agents insisted that they set up farms on the reservations, but soil there was poor and many of the crops failed.

More Land Is Opened to White Settlement

The Homestead Act, which was passed in 1862, opened land in Kansas and Nebraska for white settlement. Every head of household was permitted to claim 160 acres. Even those white settlers that moved onto land that was still in the legal possession of Native Americans could be certified as legal owners of the property. And a major push was underway to force the Native American tribes that were still free to relocate to government-controlled reservations.

When the Civil War was over, white settlers pushed even farther west. New territories were opened to white homesteaders and more soldiers were now available to deal with the Native Americans that stood in the way of white expansion.

The Native Americans who lived in the territories that were now being opened for settlement did not wish to give up their land to satisfy the demands of America's expanding white population. Even before the time that white settlements had expanded into the West, tribal leaders there had heard much about the broken promises of the United States government. They had heard about the bad, unproductive land that the United States government had issued to eastern tribes in exchange for the rich, fertile ground of their ancestral territory. Many tribal leaders in the West were determined to fight. They would band together to fight the white armies and chase back the settlers who wanted to take away their homeland.

Trespassers on Native American Land

By the mid-1860s, steam trains, as well as wagons full of white settlers and gold prospectors, headed west and routinely crossed over the Indian Territory. These strange new vehicles frightened away the buffalo, disturbed the Native Americans' livestock, and damaged their crops. When the Native Americans demanded payment for the damage white settlers caused, or tried to defend their land from this unauthorized intrusion, they were labeled as being "hostiles," and troops were often sent in to subdue or kill them.

The United States government was anxious to encourage the development of the western states. In order to protect white settlers, the government marked off trails for the wagon trains and threatened to punish any Native Americans that attacked them. Sometimes, soldiers were sent with wagon trains to ensure their security.

New Plans for Western Reservations

The invasion of whites into the West resulted in many raids and military clashes. To reduce the threat to settlers, Commissioner of Indian Affairs Luke Lea recommended that tribal territory be reduced and that western tribes be assigned to reservations, which would be located on a portion of their former territory. In an address to Congress, Lea said, "Any plan for the civilization of our Indians will, in my judgment, be fatally defective, if it does not provide for their . . . concentration [onto reserva-tions]."[2] These reservations were to be located away from white settlements and routes that whites normally traveled. Lea also suggested that Native Americans be required to stay within the boundaries of their reservation, and out of the way of white travelers and settlers.

The pattern of conquering the tribes, reducing the size of their territory, and forcing them to live on government-assigned reservations was used against tribes throughout the West. By 1856, government agents had negotiated fifty-two treaties with western tribes that forced them to live on greatly reduced portions of their former territory. Usually, the tribes were promised money and supplies if they went along with the government plan to stay on the reservations until the govern-ment determined that they could be adequately civilized to live in mainstream society.

Destruction of the Buffalo Herds

While the government was legislating new ways of pushing Native Americans off their land, some white settlers had found yet another way of making their life more difficult. They were doing their best to destroy the mighty buffalo herds that ranged across the western Plains.

Many of the western tribes, especially those who lived in the Great Plains area, depended heavily on hunting buffalo for survival. They ate the buffalo meat and used the skins for cloth-ing, tepees, and many other purposes. Hardly any part of the buffalo went to waste.

But when white settlers came into the region, they often killed buffalo only for the skin and left their meat to rot on the field. Later on, when whites realized that by eliminating the buffalo herds they could harm the tribes that depended on them, they killed buffalo for that reason alone. Some people made a sport of shooting buffalo from horseback or from railroad cars as they rode through the Great Plains.

Buffalo Bill Cody, who was later known for the spectacular "Wild West" shows he staged across the country, was one of the most famous buffalo hunters in American history. He bragged that at one time he had killed 4,280 buffalo within 17 months.[3]

Sometimes, Native Americans would find piles of buffalo rotting on the Plains. In an effort to stop these attacks on buffalo herds by whites, Native Americans tore up railroad tracks and placed huge logs over the tracks to derail the trains.

The wasteful slaughter of buffalo was the government's silent policy to cause food shortages, which would in time force the Plains tribes to live on reservations. Lieutenant General Sheridan said, "The white hide hunters have done more . . . to settle the vexing Indian question than the entire regular army has done in the past thirty years. For the sake of lasting peace, let them kill, skin, and sell until the buffalo are exterminated."[4]

The Plains tribes that depended on buffalo were furious at the efforts of whites to force their tribes onto reservations. In 1866, at a conference between Native American leaders and the United States Army near Fort Ellsworth, Kansas, Roman Nose, a chief of the southern Cheyennes, delivered the following warning to General Palmer: "We will not have the wagons which make a noise [steam engines] in the hunting grounds of the buffalo. If the palefaces come farther into our land, there will be scalps of your brethren in the wigwams of the Cheyennes. I have spoken."[5]

But his warning was not heeded. Between 1860 and 1890, thousands of white settlers continued to trespass over Native American lands, nearly wiping out the two great buffalo herds of the northern and southern Plains. At one time, nearly 15 million buffalo lived on America's Plains. The southern buffalo herd was destroyed by 1880, and by 1885 the northern herd had nearly disappeared. The disappearance of the buffalo herds caused some tribes to surrender to the government and move onto reservations.

But other tribes decided to stand their ground and fight the white settlers.

Wars with Western Tribes

Numerous wars between Native Americans and white armies broke out on account of the new push for white settlement. The United States Army engaged in more than a thousand battles with Native Americans between 1861 and 1891. These battles caused the death of more than fifty-five hundred Native Americans and more than twenty-five hundred United States soldiers. Most of the fighting took place in the Southwest and the Great Plains regions.

The discovery of gold in the Black Hills of South Dakota in 1859 triggered a new rush of prospectors and settlers that swarmed into the region. The Sioux, Cheyenne, and Arapaho tribes who lived in the Great Plains decided it was time to take action. They attacked white trespassers and destroyed the forts the government had built to protect the travelers during their journey.

Between 1860 and 1886, many bands of Apache that had not yet been forced onto reservations waged hit-and-run warfare against settlers and United States troops in New Mexico and Arizona. In 1871, the United States government decided to put an end to the Apaches' free living and force them to settle onto reservations they laid out for them in present-day Arizona and New Mexico. But these free-ranging tribes were not willing to give up their lifestyle to please the government.

Geronimo, one of the most famous Apache leaders, rallied Native Americans who were still living free in the Southwest to fight the white encroachment on their land. His forces attacked and nearly captured Fort Apache, causing the government to wage a five-year campaign against him. By the time Geronimo was forced to surrender in 1886, the government had deployed five thousand soldiers, nearly one fourth of the army, to the Southwest.

These wars prompted General William Sherman to observe in 1867, "The more [American Indians] we can kill this year, the less will have to be killed the next war, for the more I see of these Indians, the more convinced I am that they all have to be killed or be maintained as a species of paupers [forced to live on charity]."[6]

By the late 1860s, the war against the western tribes became so expensive that the United States government decided to appoint commissioners to attempt to make peace with tribes living in the West. But by then, most of the tribal leaders in the West had heard enough about the promises of the United States government to know they could not be trusted. Their only choice was to fight the whites that continued to invade their territory, or else surrender and be sent to reservations, where they could not live as they wanted and had to depend totally on government provisions for survival. So the fighting went on.

The United States Army, with its superior military power, was victorious in most of its campaigns against the natives. But despite their lack of sophisticated weapons, the Native Americans had a number of military successes. One of the best-known of these Native American victories was the Battle of the Little Bighorn in North Dakota in 1876—also known as Custer's Last Stand.

In this battle, two thousand Sioux warriors, led by Chief Crazy Horse and Chief Sitting Bull, wiped out General George Custer and the six hundred troops of his Seventh Cavalry unit. But the victory was only temporary. During the next five years, the United States government waged an all-out war against the Sioux and Cheyenne tribes to gain access to land they believed held vast quantities of gold. Finally, the tribes were forced to give up much of their beloved homeland and move onto government-controlled reservations.

By then, government policy was firmly set against the tribes remaining in the land that the United States had once promised was theirs forever. In 1880, the following statement was read in the United States Senate:

> Congress must apprise [inform] the Indian that he can no longer stand as a breakwater against the constant tide of civilization . . . An idle and thriftless race of savages cannot be permitted to stand guard at the treasure vaults of the nation which hold our gold and silver . . . the prospector and the miner may enter and by enriching himself enrich the nation and bless the world by the result of his toil.[7]

During the late 1800s, thousands of white settlers poured into North America's western region every year. The land west of the Mississippi River had been guaranteed to belong to the Native Americans forever. But once white settlers became interested in the region, all promises were forgotten. Many of the tribes that had already been forced to move far from their original homeland were compelled by the government to relocate once again.

Before the 1800s were over, the white armies had defeated nearly all of the western tribes. With little game available to hunt, most of the reservation tribes lived partly by farming or ranching, and partly from government rations. But while the government had forced the western tribes to drastically alter their way of life, they had not yet destroyed their spirit.

Chapter 7

LIFE ON RESERVATIONS

Even after Native Americans moved to reservations, the United States government did not permit them to live in their own way. The government wanted to have control over their lifestyles and activities. In this way, government leaders felt, they could eventually civilize the Native Americans to the point that they could be brought into the mainstream of American society.[1] One goal of the civilization process was to abolish traditional Native American leadership and cause tribe members to look to the authority of the United States government instead.

The traditional forms of government of Native American tribes were simple but effective. Vine Deloria, Jr., and Clifford Lytle, authors of *The Nations Within: The Past and Future of American Indian Sovereignty*, described it in this way:

> Because the tribes understood their place in the universe as one given specifically to them, they had no need to evolve special political institutions to shape and order their society. A council at which everyone could speak, a council to remind the people of their sacred obligations to the cosmos and to themselves, was sufficient for most purposes.[2]

Such a system of tribal government served the needs of the native population well. But it did not serve the needs of the United States government to keep the tribes under their control and to direct them towards the "civilized" life they wanted Native Americans to lead.

The Government Sends Agents to the Tribes

In 1832, the United States government created the Indian Office, which was to be responsible for the government's relations with the Native American tribes. The Indian Office appointed a white person as an "Indian agent" to oversee the operation of every reservation.

The duties of an Indian agent were to enforce reservation rules and distribute food and other provisions that were sent to the tribes by the government. These appointments were often made as political favors. Some Native Americans were appointed as judges. Others were selected to be members of the reservation police. But the people who made the rules, gave the final decisions, and oversaw the operation of the reservation were always white.

Corruption quickly became rampant throughout the program. Indian agents often helped themselves to the provisions the government sent to them for the tribes' use.

During this time, most reservations were virtual concentration camps. The laws of many reservations required Native Americans to stay within reservation boundaries and live on the inadequate provisions provided by the government.

As word got out about conditions on the reservations, some political and religious leaders in the East became concerned. In 1867, a group of people, known as the Indian Peace Commission, were appointed to examine the problem. They discovered that many of the agents had defrauded the Native Americans they were supposed to be helping. The agents often kept a large part of the money for themselves, and used whatever remained to buy spoiled food and poor quality goods to deliver to the tribes. The Indian Peace Commission revealed in its report:

> The records are abundant to show that agents have pocketed the funds appropriated by the government and driven the Indians to starvation. It cannot be doubted that Indian wars have originated from this cause. The Sioux War, in Minnesota, is supposed to have been produced in this way. For a long time these officers have been selected from the partisan ranks, not so much on account of honesty and qualification as devotion to party interests and the willingness to apply the money of the Indian to promote the selfish schemes of local politicians.[3]

The report came as shock to many Americans. As a result of this report, some opportunities for corruption in the system were corrected. But many opportunities for corruption still remained and the United States government's plan to civilize Native Americans by separating them from their cultural heritage continued.

Educating Native American Children

One of the government's methods of civilizing the Native Americans was to teach their children English and give them a "white" education. This, government officials felt, would make the children want to give up their traditional native lifestyle and voluntarily assimilate themselves into the white world.

But Native Americans had realized early on that a white person's education did not give their children the skills they needed to live in the traditional ways of their ancestors. When the Virginia Legislature offered to send six Native American youth to be educated at the College of William and Mary in 1744, a member of the Iroquois League had this reply:

> Several of our young People were formerly brought up in the colleges of the Northern Provinces; they were

instructed in all your Sciences; but when they came back to us, they were bad Runners, ignorant of every means of living in the woods, unable to bear either cold or hunger, knew neither how to build a Cabin, take a deer, or kill an enemy, spoke our language imperfectly, were therefore neither fit for Hunters, Warriors nor Counsellors; they were totally good for nothing.[4]

But despite complaints from Native American leaders that a white education was not useful for reservation life, the decision had been made.

By the mid-1800s, schools had been established on many reservations. Most were operated by government agencies or religious groups. The reservation children were taught how to speak and write the English language, and were trained in skills, such as sewing, carpentry, and metalwork, that could be used in white society.

But as soon as the reservation children returned home from their lessons, they spoke their native language and practiced tribal customs with their families. So the government's next move in separating Native American children from their traditional ways was to send them away to white-operated boarding schools.

One of the first boarding schools established for this purpose was the Carlisle Indian Industrial School. It was located in a former army base in Carlisle, Pennsylvania. The school, founded by Lieutenant Richard Harry Pratt, first opened in 1879. In 1882, the United States government expanded the program by authorizing that abandoned military forts and stockades across the country could be used as boarding schools for Native American children. Three years later, 177 of these schools were in operation.

Very few Native American parents wanted their children to be taken to a boarding school far away from the reservation. When the government agents found that tribal leaders would not cooperate with their plan, the children were often removed by force.

Being separated from their tribe was a very traumatic experience for Native American children. They were taken away from everything they had known and put in the hands of white strangers who they did not trust.

In boarding schools, Native Americans were usually forbidden to speak their tribal languages or to practice native religions. They were forced to wear white styles of clothing, and the boys were forced to have their hair cut short in white men's fashion. In many cases, Native American children were required to adopt white names in place of the name their parents gave them. Regulations at the boarding schools were so severe that some Native American children tried to run away and return to the tribe.

Lone Wolf, a member of the Blackfoot tribe, described his experiences of being taken away to boarding school:

> The soldiers came and rounded up as many of the Blackfeet children as they could. . . . None of us wanted to go and our parents didn't want to let us go. Oh, we cried for this was the first time we were to be separated from our parents. . . . Once there our belongings were taken from us, even the little medicine bag our mothers had given us to protect us from harm. Everything was placed in a heap and set afire.[5]

White diseases, such as measles, smallpox and tuberculosis, which Native Americans had no immunity to, were a serious threat to children attending white-operated boarding schools. Many became ill and died. Even those students who were able to adapt to life at boarding school did not have an easy life. Once they had finished school, they felt out of place in both Native American and white societies.[6]

The skills the Native American children learned at boarding school often had no value on reservations. Because they had spent so much of their youth at the boarding school, Native American children returning to the tribe did not have the skills necessary to live in the traditional way.

Boarding school graduates who tried to live in the white world were also at a disadvantage. Because they were Native Americans, they were not readily accepted by white society. Also, the skills Native Americans were taught in most boarding schools only prepared them for employment at menial, low-paying jobs.

So while some Native American boarding school graduates were successful at adapting to life in the white world, many more were literally lost between the world of white society and the world of Native America.

The Government Bans Native Religions

Persuading Native Americans to convert to Christianity had always been an important part of the civilization program whites imposed on the reservation tribes. But despite many decades of work by missionaries, the program had only limited success. Finally, the United States government decided to pass laws designed to put an end to all traditional Native American religious practices.

In 1883, Secretary of the Interior Henry M. Teller established the "court of Indian offenses" to deal with this issue. Secretary Teller, as well as the Christian religious organizations that backed him, hoped that the new laws would eliminate the "heathenish practices" they found so distasteful.

The new laws, which first went into effect during the 1880s and 1890s, stated that any Native American engaging in the practice of their ancestral religion should be punished by withholding government rations or by serving time in prison.

In 1904, the Bureau of Indian Affairs published an official list of the rules and penalties that stated:

> The "Sun Dance" and all other similar dances and so-called religious ceremonies shall be considered "Indian offenses," and any Indian found guilty of being a participant in any one or more of these offenses shall . . . be punished by withholding his rations for a period of not exceeding ten days: and if found guilty of any subsequent offense under this rule, shall be punished by withholding his rations for a period of not less than fifteen days nor more than thirty days, or by incarceration in the agency prison for a period not exceeding thirty days.[7]

The Court of Indian Offenses gave even more severe punishments to Native American spiritual leaders:

> The usual practices of so-called "medicine men" shall be considered "Indian offenses" . . . [punishable by confinement] in the agency guardhouse for a term not less than ten days, or until such times as he shall produce evidence satisfactory to the court, and approved by the agent, that he will forever abandon all practices styled Indian offenses under this rule.[8]

But despite the government's threats, these rules did not stop all Native American religious practices. There were not enough enforcement officers to monitor or control it.

Other tribal traditions also came under attack from the new reservation laws. Some tribes, for example, had permitted men to have more than one wife. Quanah Parker, chief of the Quahadi Comanches, was one Native American who was affected by this ordinance. When informed about this new regulation, he said:

> A long time ago I lived free among the buffalo on the Staked Plains and had as many wives as I wanted,

according to the laws of my people. I used to go to war in Texas and Mexico. You wanted me to stop fighting and sent messages all the time: "You stop, Quanah. You come here. You sit down, Quanah." You did not say anything then, "How many wives you got, Quanah?"[9]

It was during this period that a new Native American religion, known as the Ghost Dance religion, spread rapidly among western Sioux tribes. The Ghost Dance was taught by Wovoka, a religious leader of the Paiute tribe who claimed to be the Messiah. He promised Native Americans that if they believed in this new religion and kept up the dance, all of their dead family members and ancestors, as well as the buffalo, would return to the earth. It also promised that the whites, who had taken over their land, would be destroyed. The Ghost Dance religion offered hope to reservation tribes, and many sent their holy men to Nevada to hear Wovoka and learn more about it.

The government, fearing that Ghost Dancing had something to do with a planned military uprising, tried to suppress this new religion. They threatened to arrest anyone that taught or practiced it. In 1889, Sioux Chief Sitting Bull said of this policy, "Our religion seems foolish to you, but so does yours to me. . . . Why does this agent seek to take away our religion? . . . If this new religion [Ghost Dance] is not true then what does it matter?"[10]

Native Americans who practiced the Ghost Dance religion believed that as long as they wore their specially painted Ghost Dance shirts, the bullets of the white soldiers could not harm them.[11] So they danced on in defiance of the law. This made the army officials even more nervous. They sent a telegraph that said "Indians are dancing in the snow and are wild and crazy,"[12] and requested military enforcement.

As time went on, the government's fears about Native Americans practicing the Ghost Dance religion intensified. They were afraid that believers in this religion might suddenly decide to wage war against the whites. This fear by government and military officials led to one of the worst massacres of Native Americans in the nation's history.

Wounded Knee

On December 29, 1890, a group of 106 Sioux warriors that were camped at Wounded Knee were ordered by the U.S. Army to give up their guns. These warriors, who believed in the Ghost Dance religion, were part of a group of 350 Sioux that were being moved to a reservation in Omaha.

As the soldiers searched through the warriors' belongings, a gun accidentally went off. This triggered shooting on both sides, and was the beginning of one of the worst massacres of Native Americans. The soldiers fired repeatedly on the Native Americans, not stopping to see if their guns were aimed at armed warriors, or were pointed instead at unarmed Sioux families who were also at the camp. When the shooting was over, approximately three hundred Native Americans and twenty-five United States soldiers had been killed. Many Sioux women, children, and elderly were massacred during the attack.

This was a very dark time in the history of Native Americans. With their traditional way of life intentionally being destroyed by their white conquerors, many Native Americans became demoralized. They could no longer live as they had before the arrival of the European settlers, and they were pressured at every turn to give up all that their people held sacred.

And still, the United States government wanted to take more land from them.

Chapter 8

LEGISLATION TAKES MORE NATIVE AMERICAN LAND

As the United States' white population continued to grow, so did the demand for land. By the late 1800s, the United States' white population had reached nearly 70 million, and the bulk of North American land that had once belonged to the native population was now in the hands of white owners.

But still, there was a great demand for opening more land to white settlement. Politicians in the West were especially anxious for Congress to open more tribal land in their area for white settlement and development. So America's political leaders, in an effort to please voters, began to formulate new policies that would take even more land away from Native Americans.

The Government Breaks Up Tribal Homelands

During this time, a humanitarian group in the East known as "Friends of the Indian" formulated a plan that they felt would help to civilize the tribes. They believed that private property ownership was the key to instilling the values of civilization in Native Americans. So they proposed that reservation lands be broken up into tracts and assigned to individual tribe members.

This, they felt, would cause the Native Americans to want to be farmers or raise livestock and live like white Americans.[1]

The private ownership of property, which was common throughout Europe and white America, was totally foreign to the way that most Native Americans lived—which was to communally farm, hunt, and move from place to place as conditions warranted.

Unlike typical white communities of the time, many tribal villages functioned much like an extended family. The women, men, and children of a Native village lived and worked together like a group of close relatives. To separate these villages into individual families that lived on separate plots of land, sometimes far removed from each other, forced them to drastically alter their way of life. Breaking up the reservations was more than an assault on what remained of Native American land—it was an assault on their culture as well.

The Omaha Treaty, which was passed in 1854, was the model for this plan. It was the first treaty to include private land ownership and farming as a provision. In part, the treaty stated:

> And if any such person or family shall at any time neglect or refuse to occupy and till a portion of the land assigned, and on which they have located, or shall rove from place to place, the President may, if the patent shall have been issued, revoke the same, or if not issued, cancel the assignment, and may also withhold from such person or family, their proportion of the annuities [which were to be paid to the members for the land they had already given up] or other moneys due them, until they shall have returned to such permanent home, and resumed the pursuits of industry; and in default of their return, the tract may be declared abandoned, and thereafter assigned to some other person or family of such confederated tribes, or disposed of as is provided for the disposal of the excess of said land.[2]

The Omaha Treaty, as well as others that followed, forced the concept of private land ownership on tribes that no longer had the military power to resist the government's terms. Such treaties, through their skillfully worded provisions, made it possible for the United States government to take even more land away from the Native Americans.

According to the agreement, any lands that were not assigned to an individual Native American or farmed as the government required could be taken away from Native American control. These lands were considered by the government to be "surplus" or "abandoned." They were sold to immigrant settlers or opened up to homesteading by white American settlers from the East Coast.

Such treaties were especially hard on Plains tribes who had existed mostly by hunting buffalo, and had little or no knowledge of farming methods. Many of these tribes had no seeds or farm machinery with which to attempt to grow crops. When government inspectors saw that tracts of land were not being used as the law required, they were able to legally take it away from the tribe forever.

General Allotment Act

Dividing tribal land into parcels became standard government policy in 1887 when the General Allotment Act, also known as the Dawes Severalty Act, was passed into law. Shortly after its approval, most Native American reservations were subdivided into tracts.

Each family head was to receive a 160-acre tract and every single person over eighteen was to receive an 80-acre tract. The United States government was to hold the title to these parcels of land for twenty-five years. Once that time period was up, Native American owners could sell it if they wished.

After land allotments were issued to all eligible tribal members, the United States government purchased any tracts that remained at a tiny fraction of their true worth. The government purchased many of these tracts for $1.25 per acre. Then, they resold them to white settlers for $2.50 an acre. Part of the money the government collected for this land was deposited in the United States Treasury. The rest of was distributed on a per-person basis to Native Americans.

Results of the General Allotment Act

The General Allotment Act profoundly affected the way many Native Americans lived. The traditional way of life Native Americans were used to was no longer possible in the limited space the General Allotment Act permitted them. A petition to Congress from the Five Civilized Tribes said:

> Our people have not asked for or authorized this [allotment], for the reason that they believe it could do no good and would only result in misheif in our present condition . . . At least two thirds of our country is suitable only for grazing purposes. No man can afford to live by stock-raising and hearding who is restricted to 160 or even 320 acres, especially on lands away from water.[3]

Out of economic necessity, many Native Americans had to lease their land allotment to white farmers and ranchers. This, in effect, took that parcel of land out of Native American hands and brought white settlers onto the reservations.

Not long after the General Allotment Act was passed, things began to disintegrate rapidly. White settlers moved onto land that had been declared surplus or was leased to them by Native American owners. They cleared the land to set up farms and towns. This made less land available for Native Americans, as well as for the animals their people had traditionally hunted for food.

As a result of this legislation, Native Americans were forced to learn new ways of living in order to survive. Some Native

Americans decided to try to make a living farming the plot of land that was allotted to them. But this was extremely difficult, since the government provided only $1.62 per tract for seeds, equipment, supplies, and livestock.

Other Native Americans chose to become educated in the ways of the white people and learn to live in their economic system. Some were able to make a living working in towns near reservations. Others, especially young people that had attended boarding schools in distant cities, chose to remain in those cities after their graduation. But leaving their tribe behind and working in white society was not an easy decision for many Native Americans. Even though they were now permitted to leave the reservations, decades of forced segregation made them feel that they would be unwelcome among whites.

The program created numerous controversies, and a whole new class of government bureaucrats was created to deal with them. During the years that the General Allotment Act was in effect, Native Americans lost control of more than 90 million acres of their land.[4] Most of those tracts were lost to the tribes through fraudulent dealings of the United States government, business interests, and private citizens.[5]

The Meriam Report Exposes Government Fraud

In 1926, the secretary of the Interior, Hubert Work, commissioned a study of the conditions on reservations. This study, which came to be known as the Meriam Report, was published two years later. The 872-page report documented the terrible situation on reservations. These appalling conditions included widespread food shortages, poor health, high mortality rates, inadequate housing, and a lack of education.

The writers of the Meriam Report declared that the United States government's efforts to assimilate the Native Americans had been a total failure. They recommended that an end be put to the allotment program, that more funds be made available for Native American health and education programs, and that the Bureau of Indian Affairs, which the United States government had created in 1824 to oversee the operation of the reservations, hire Native Americans as employees.

Indian Reorganization Act

The Meriam Report led government leaders to seriously reevaluate the nation's policy toward Native Americans. John Collier, who was appointed commissioner of Indian Affairs by President Franklin D. Roosevelt in 1933, also did much to bring the conditions Native Americans were living under to national attention. The Indian Reorganization Act, passed in 1934 during the Roosevelt administration, was the direct result of his concern. It was a dramatic shift in government policy toward Native Americans.

The Indian Reorganization Act called for a halt to the allotment of tribal lands. It also restored many of the important freedoms that the government had taken from the Native Americans. It guaranteed the natives the right to practice traditional religions and lifestyles, free from government interference.

The Indian Reorganization Act proposed that tribes organize their governments under tribal constitutions, and contained provisions that encouraged economic development and self-determination for the tribes. But despite its many benefits, the act did not totally restore the Native Americans' right to handle their own affairs. The Bureau of Indian Affairs still had to give their approval before many tribal government decisions could be legally put into effect.

Still, the Indian Reorganization Act was a major turning point for Native Americans. It gave them back some of the dignity they had lost under previous administrations.

Termination Policy

By the early 1950s, the political tide was again beginning to turn against Native Americans. Since the mid-1940s, America had experienced unprecedented urban and industrial expansion. To provide for this rapid expansion, the U.S. Congress was again pressured to open more Native American land for white development.

During this time, some United States government officials felt that financing Bureau of Indian Affairs programs for the reservations had become too much of a burden. To limit the rising expense of the programs and make Native American land and natural resources such as minerals, timber, water, and energy resources available to the non-native population, they decided that the best way to deal with the country's native population was to quickly assimilate them into the general population.

Some members of Congress determined that the best way to accomplish this was to abolish government services to the tribes. They wanted to "liberate" Native Americans from Bureau of Indian Affairs programs, abolish tribal governments, and terminate all federal responsibility for the welfare of Native Americans. These congresspeople also wanted to put an end to the health services, education, and other benefits that the Indian Reorganization Act had provided to the tribes.[6]

The House Concurrent Resolution 108, passed in 1953, was the beginning of this effort. It said:

> It is the policy of the Congress, as rapidly as possible, to make the Indians within the United States subject to the same laws and entitled to the same privileges and responsibilities as are applicable to other citizens of the United States, to end their status as wards of the United States, and to grant them all of the rights and prerogatives pertaining to American Citizenship.[7]

The Indian Termination and Relocation Acts, which were passed during the 1950s, dissolved all or parts of 109 Native American tribal nations. The Termination Policy, however, was not as popular as the government leaders that formulated it had hoped. The policy received a strong negative reaction from Native Americans, the general public, and many members of Congress.

Part of the Termination and Relocation program was to encourage Native Americans, especially the tribe's youth, to leave reservations by offering money and education to those who agreed to relocate to urban areas. They wanted Native Americans to get an education in the ways of white society, work in the general economy, and leave their tribes and cultural traditions behind.

The Bureau of Indian Affairs set up a Relocation Division in 1952 to assist in this effort. It was named the Employment Assistance Program. The program offered education and financial rewards to Native Americans that left reservations and moved to cities. In 1957, the Bureau of Indian Affairs set up the Adult Vocational Training program to encourage more Native Americans to learn marketable skills that could be used in the white world.

As of 1960, these programs had encouraged more than thirty-five thousand Native Americans to leave the reservations for cities such as Los Angeles, Chicago, Denver, and Oklahoma City. But within a few years, 35 percent of those Native Americans decided to return to the reservations.[8]

The 1960s Bring New Government Policies

During the 1960s, another major change occurred in federal policy. The official government policy towards Native Americans shifted away from termination and focused on economic and political self-determination for the tribes.

Many of these changes were brought about by government investigations of living conditions on the reservations. In 1961, after receiving numerous complaints, Secretary of the Interior Stewart Udall appointed a task force to investigate the conditions of reservations. The task force found that most Native Americans were living in poverty, and many did not have adequate food, health care, housing, or educational services. The study also determined that termination policies had "impaired Indian moral and produced a hostile or apathetic response" to federal programs.[9] Other studies of reservations conducted during the 1960s had similar findings.

President Lyndon Johnson was very concerned about conditions on the reservations. He said, "We must affirm the right of the first Americans to remain Indians . . . [and] their right to freedom of choice and self-determination."[10] Many of the programs Johnson enacted during his administration to fight poverty on a national level helped Native Americans, who at the time were among the poorest citizens in the country. During Johnson's term in office, more federal money than ever before was sent to help Native Americans with urgent needs such as housing, education, health care, and attracting industry to the area to provide jobs.

A few years later, President Richard Nixon reassured the country's Native American population of continued federal support of the tribes by saying: "And we must make clear that Indians can become independent of Federal control without being cut off from Federal concern and Federal support."[11]

The new positive changes in the United States government's relations with the Native American tribes did not happen by itself. They were the result of decades of relentless work by Native Americans involved in numerous organizations who had strived to bring issues involving Native American rights to public and government attention.

RESERVATIONS TODAY

Reservations today are a mixture of the past and the present. While reservations hold the traditional culture of the Native American people, at the same time they embrace many of the advantages of the white world. Reservations differ greatly from each other. They differ in size, population, land quality, and ecological makeup.

While no Native American is required to stay on a reservation by the United States government, many choose to do so. The reservation is what remains of the tribe's original estate. Living there among other members of their own tribe gives Native Americans a sense of community. On the reservations, they can enjoy the customs and traditions of their tribe while living among their own people.

Beasley Denson, the secretary/treasurer of the Choctaw Tribal Council had this comment about living with his tribe: "I like living in this community, and I like being Choctaw, but that's all there is to it. Just because I don't want to be a white man doesn't mean I want to be some kind of mystical Indian either. Just a real human being."[1]

According to the 1990 census, about 35 percent of Native Americans live on or near reservations. The rest live in cities, towns, and rural areas.

Native America in the 1990s

The number of Native Americans in the United States is on the increase. As of 1990, the Native American population of the United States is about 2 million. No one knows exactly how many Native Americans were here at the time that Columbus discovered America. But many experts think this might be the highest population figure for Native Americans since Europeans began to colonize the nation.

Currently, more than three hundred reservations are recognized by the United States government. Some of these reservations are occupied by only one tribe of Native Americans, while others are shared. The Native American land base in the United States currently encompasses about 54 million acres. That is about 2 percent of the land mass of the continental United States. This figure includes federally recognized reservations, as well as rancherias, native villages, colonies, Native American trust lands, and historic Native American areas.

Reservation Government

For several decades, most reservations have been governed primarily by elected tribal leaders. These leaders are voted into office by tribal members. Most reservation governments operate under the guidelines of tribal constitutions, which were approved by the tribes in the mid-1930s shortly after the Indian Reorganization Act was passed.

Because of the special legal status of reservations, some state and federal laws apply to activities within a reservation, while others do not. United States federal courts have generally affirmed tribal leaders' rights to make decisions in civil matters and cases involving minor crimes. The federal government, however, has jurisdiction over serious crimes such as murder, manslaughter, rape, larceny, and arson.

Keeping Native American Culture Alive

Cultural traditions play an important role in the lives of many Native Americans. Even Native Americans who live far away from their tribe's reservation find ways of keeping in touch with their tribal culture. Powwows are one of the most popular ways for Native Americans to celebrate their cultural roots. Marty Kreipe, a member of the Potawatome tribe, said, "We move around, leave the [reservation, but] we come back at pow-wow times or celebrations. Then we need our own things just as much as in the past."[2]

The Red Earth Festival held in Oklahoma is the largest powwow in the nation. Native Americans from all tribes are invited to come and participate in dance contests, art shows, Native American music, parades, and many other events.

Native Americans have created cultural centers in over a dozen cities across the country. Some large cities, such as Los Angeles, New York, San Francisco, Phoenix, and Seattle, have a large enough Native American population to form social, cultural, and religious groups. In addition to furnishing Native American residents with a place to meet, their offerings include galleries of Native American art, gift shops for selling Native American crafts, and outreach programs to explain Native American culture to the general public.

Many reservations have their own media outlets. Dozens of tribes publish newspapers that keep their readers informed about events in the Native American community. Also, in the past few decades, some tribes have started operating their own radio stations. These media outlets give Native Americans dependable sources of information, as well as a voice in the events and issues that affect their lives.

High-stakes Casinos

Reservations vastly differ in the economic opportunities available to tribal members who live there. Some of the more financially successful tribes have made tremendous profits by operating high-stakes casinos on their reservations. Since the 1980s, more than a hundred tribes in over twenty states have opened casinos or other forms of gambling halls on their reservations. The funds raised from gambling have helped to replace those lost by the drastic federal budget cutbacks of the 1980s. Casinos serve to provide a sense of independence for tribes, as well as employment opportunities for Native Americans who might otherwise be forced to live on welfare.

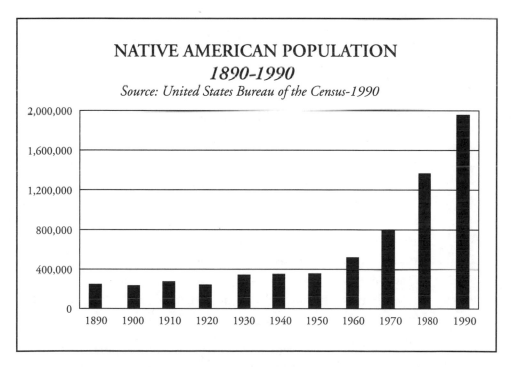

The Native American population in the United States grew rapidly from 1890 to 1990. And by 2010 they numbered almost 3 million.

The profits from operating gambling halls can be astounding. Reservation gambling is estimated to raise a total of over $2.5 billion a year. Each tribal government makes its own decisions as to how the money is used. It can be divided among tribal members, put into public works projects, or used for other beneficial purposes.

Casino income often makes it possible for reservations to fund projects and programs they could not otherwise afford. One band of Chippewa, the Mille Lacs, decided to use their casino profits to finance $20 million in construction projects that include a school, a health clinic, a day-care unit, and a water system.

However, quite a bit of controversy still surrounds the use of casino gambling to raise revenue for tribes. Some state governments object to reservations located within their states running gambling operations that they have no control over.

This controversy led to Congress passing the Indian Gaming Regulatory Act in 1988. Once this law was passed, any state that permitted any form of gambling, even if it was only permitted for charitable purposes, could not forbid Native American tribes to operate the same games on their reservations for profit.

But the controversy is far from over. Even within the tribes, not all Native American leaders agree that the windfall profits generated by casinos is the best economic direction for their people to take. While the money generated from gambling is certainly welcome, casinos have also had some negative effects on the tribes.

In a letter to the *Lakota Times* on January 21, 1992, Wallace Wells, Jr., of the Crow Creek Sioux tribe said:

I am writing in regard to the No. 1 issue in Indian country . . . Our tribe has been in a tumult because of the issue of gambling. It has brought out the worst in people. Such as power hungry leaders who have sold themselves out to greed . . . As a tribal leader, I have never been bothered so much in my life by people who want to invest in our tribe—for gambling.[3]

Income of Reservation Families

While casino gambling has received a great deal of press attention in recent years, it is certainly not the only means of economic growth open to reservations. Native Americans have found many other ways to prosper. Mining, farming, ranching, timber cutting, high technology, and Native American arts and crafts are among the leading income producers of the 1990s.

In a 1990 study, it was found that 46,200 Native American families and groups earned their living through farming or ranching, producing a total income of over $400 million a year. Income from oil and gas taken from Native American land, another lucrative income producer, generates over $80 million per year.

Native American arts and crafts, another important source of income, have seen a surge in popularity in recent years. At the retail level, they generate several hundred million dollars in retail sales annually. But since most of the retail market is still controlled by non-Native Americans, only a portion of that money actually reaches the native artists and craftspeople.

While the residents of some reservations have had great financial success, others live in poverty. On average, Native American families living on a reservation make 40 percent less income a year than the average white family. Nearly one third of the total Native American population lives below the poverty line. A few reservations have an unemployment rate of up to 80 percent, forcing many of their residents to depend on welfare and food stamps to survive. This lack of economic opportunity has led to higher than average rates of alcoholism and suicide in the Native American population.

Government Services for Native Americans

Native Americans today receive a wide variety of important services from the United States government. One of the main agencies that provides these services is the Bureau of Indian Affairs. The BIA assists the tribes in such areas as economic aid, health care, housing programs, education, and natural resource development and management, as well as many other programs. Their budget for 1995 was $1.7 billion. Today, more than 80 percent of Bureau of Indian Affairs employees are Native Americans.

Many Bureau of Indian Affairs programs are based on the interests and needs of the tribes. These services can include such things as administrating education programs, road construction, agricultural programs, social services, and law enforcement. The BIA also manages the government's trust fund for Native American tribes, valued at approximately $2 billion.

Aside from the Bureau of Indian Affairs, the Indian Health Service (IHS) is one of the United States government's most important services to the tribes. The IHS, which is a branch of the U.S. Public Health Service, was created to give Native Americans access to high-quality health care they might not otherwise have. The Indian Health Service currently operates 50 hospitals and 450 outpatient clinics throughout the nation.

Native American Education Today

New opportunities for education, funded by the Bureau of Indian Affairs and the Education Department, is one important factor in helping tribes to overcome the problems of poverty. The passage of the Indian Education Act of 1972 and the Indian Self-Determination and Assistance Act of 1975 gave Native Americans much greater control over schools on their reservations. These two acts established a fund for multicultural and multilingual programs, the training and hiring of teachers and counselors, and the purchase of necessary educational materials. They also required that the tribes be allowed to participate in decisions affecting the education of their children.

Under the Indian Self-Determination and Education Act, tribes are encouraged to set up and operate their own schools with Bureau of Indian Affairs funding. So far, more than fifty tribes have done this.

The Bureau of Indian Affairs now contracts with the tribes to operate more than sixty day schools and eleven on-reservation boarding schools. The Bureau of Indian Affairs also helps to fund public schools that have Native American students in attendance. Every year, just about fifteen thousand students attend colleges or universities on Bureau of Indian Affairs scholarships.

Satellites, computers, and other high-tech means of communication are now being used to deliver a modern education to even the most isolated tribes. The Native American Network, based in Arizona, is a central point in this new program. Its computers link together schools, teachers, and students from Native American communities all over the nation.

In addition to bringing information about the outside world to reservations, the new technology is also being used to teach Native American children about their own heritage. The Zuni tribe in New Mexico, for example, uses computers to help teach students attending reservation schools about their native culture and language.[4]

Looking to the Future

Reservations still have many problems that have not been solved. However, conditions are gradually improving. Wilma Mankiller, Cherokee National Principal Chief, reflected this spirit of hope when she said:

> Despite facing virtually every social indicator of decline, tribal communities and individual people have a

tremendous strength, resiliency, and hope for the future. Even in the most troubled tribal communities, I hear discussions of plans for the future so that someday we will again have whole, healthy communities for our children and our children's children.[5]

☆ TIMELINE ☆

1492—Columbus lands in the West Indies.

1540—The Spanish come into North America from Mexico and begin their invasion of Pueblo tribes.

1607—The British establish their first successful North American colony in Jamestown, Virginia.

1622—The Powhatans revolt against the British settlers at Jamestown, Virginia.

1636—Pequot War against British settlers in New England begins.

1638—The first reservation is created when the Quinnipiac tribe sells land to the English colonists in New Haven, Connecticut.

1682—The Delaware tribe makes a treaty of friendship with Quaker leader William Penn.

1754-1763—The French and Indian War divides the allegiance of Native American tribes between the French and English.

1763—The British Government issues a proclamation forbidding whites to settle on land west of the Appalachian Mountains.

1775-1783—The American Revolution occurs; most Native American tribes side with England.

1787—The Northwest Ordinance is passed by Congress.

1802-1820s—The United States government attempts to persuade all eastern tribes to move west of the Mississippi.

1813—Shawnee warrior and chief Tecumseh sides with the British to fight against America's colonial government.

1824—The United States government creates the Bureau of Indian Affairs as a part of the War Department.

1830–1838—The Indian Removal Act forces 92 percent of Native Americans in the eastern part of the United States to relocate west of the Mississippi.

1861–1865—The Civil War occurs; many tribes in the East and Midwest become involved when they are forced to choose sides.

1862—The Homestead Act allows whites to settle on Native American land in Kansas and Nebraska.

1864—The beginning of the Navajo Long Walk. The United States Army forces nearly eight thousand Navajos to march more than three hundred fifty miles from their home in Arizona to a reservation in New Mexico.

1867—The United States buys Alaska from Russia, adding the Inuit and Aleut peoples to the country's Native American population.

1870—The Ghost Dance religion is founded in Nevada.

1871—Congress ends treaty making with Native American tribes.

1876—Sioux and Cheyenne warriors defeat General Custer at Little Bighorn, Montana.

1879—Captain Pratt founds the Carlisle Indian School in Pennsylvania to "civilize" Native American children.

1880s—Buffalo herds on the Great Plains are nearly exterminated by white settlers.

1887—The General Allotment Act breaks up reservation land and divides it among families and individuals.

1890—More than three hundred Sioux are massacred by American troops at Wounded Knee, South Dakota.

1934—The Indian Reorganization Act (Wheeler-Howard Act) is signed into law.

1952–1957—The Bureau of Indian Affairs starts a relocation program that moves seventeen thousand Native Americans to cities across the United States.

1953—The U.S. Congress votes to terminate the government's special relationship with tribes and attempts to dissolve reservations.

1960s—Congress is pressured to reverse its termination policy and recognize many of the Native American tribes that were terminated in the previous decade.

1971—The Native American Rights Fund is founded to provide legal representation to Native Americans in court.

1972—About five hundred Native Americans occupy the Bureau of Indian Affairs in Washington, D.C., to protest the "Trail of Broken Treaties" and to demand reforms.

1972—The Indian Education Act is passed.

1975—The Indian Self-Determination and Assistance Act is passed.

1978—The American Indian Religious Freedom Act is passed.

1988—The U.S. Supreme Court upholds the right of Native Americans to run gambling casinos on their reservations.

2004—National Museum of the American Indian (NMAI) opens at the National Mall in Washington, D.C.

☆ CHAPTER NOTES ☆

Chapter 1. This Land Was Their Land

1. Helen Jackson, *A Century of Dishonor* (New York: Indian Head Books, 1994), p. 199.

2. Ibid.

3. Ibid., p. 200.

4. Ibid.

5. Ibid.

6. Ibid., p. 201.

7. Ibid., p. 203.

8. Washington Irving, *The Rocky Mountains, or Scenes, Incidents and Adventures from the Far West, digested from the Journal of Captain B.L.E. Bonneville, of the Army of the United States, and Illustrated from Various Other Sources*, vol. I (Philadelphia: Carey, Lea, & Blanchard, 1837), in Alvin M. Josephy, Jr., *500 Nations—An Illustrated History of North American Indians* (New York: Alfred A. Knopf, 1994), pp. 18–19

9. Francis Jennings, *The Invasion of America: Indians, Colonialism, and the Cant of Conquest* (New York: W.W. Norton & Company, 1976), p. 135.

10. Fredrick Webb Hodge, ed., *Handbook of American Indians North of Mexico—Part 2* (Washington, D.C.: Washington Government Printing Office/Smithsonian Institution's Bureau of American Ethnology, 1910), p. 372.

Chapter 2. Early Relations with European Settlers

1. Robert T. Coulter and Steven M. Tullberg, "Indian Land Rights," in Sandra L. Cadwalader and Vine Deloria, Jr., eds., *The Aggressions of Civilization: Federal Indian Policy Since the 1880s* (Philadelphia: Temple University Press, 1984), pp. 185–213.

2. Alvin M. Josephy, Jr., *500 Nations—An Illustrated History of North American Indians* (New York: Alfred A. Knopf, 1994), p. 140.

3. L.G. Tyler, ed., *Narratives of Early Virginia* (New York: Barnes and Noble, 1959) in Virgil J. Vogel, *This Country Was Ours: A Documentary History of the American Indian* (New York: Harper & Row Publishers, 1972), p. 39.

4. William Bradford, *Of Plymouth Plantation*, ed. Harvey Wish (New York: Capricorn Books, 1962) in Virgil J. Vogel, *This Country Was Ours: A Documentary of the American Indian* (New York: Harper & Row Publishers, 1972), p. 41.

5. Ibid., p. 40.

Chapter 3. As the Colonies Grew

1. David E. Stannard, *American Holocaust: The Conquest of the New World* (New York: Oxford University Press, 1992), p. 109.

2. Arlene Hirschfelder and Martha Kreipe de Montano, *The Native American Almanac* (New York: Prentice Hall General Reference, 1993), p. 3.

3. Arrell Morgan Gibson, *The American Indian—Prehistory to Present* (Toronto: D.C. Heath and Company, 1980), p. 191.

4. Ibid., p. 193.

5. Ibid., pp. 195–196.

Chapter 4. Native American Involvement in White Wars

1. Angie Debo, *A History of the Indians of the United States* (Norman, Okla.: University of Oklahoma Press, 1970), p. 65.

2. Henry S. Commager, ed., *Documents of American History* (New York: Appleton-Century-Crofts, 1968), pp. 47–50.

3. Virgil J. Vogel, *This Country Was Ours: A Documentary History of the American Indian* (New York: Harper and Row Publishers, 1972), p. 65.

4. Gibson, p. 261.

5. Ibid., p. 259.

6. Ibid., p. 262.

7. Kirke Kickingbird and Karen Ducheneaux, *One Hundred Million Acres* (New York: Macmillan Publishing Company, 1973), xxviii–xxiv.

8. Gibson, p. 266.

9. Tecumseh, *Touch the Earth: A Self-Portrait of Indian Existence*, ed. T.C. McLuhan (New York: Promontory Press, 1971), p. 69.

10. Debo, p. 93.

11. Howard Zinn, *A People's History of the United States* (New York: Harper Perennial, 1990), p. 127.

Chapter 5. Native American Removal Policy

1. Herman Melville, *The Confidence Man* (New York: Hendricks House, 1954) in Virgil J. Vogel, *This Country Was Ours: A Documentary History of the American Indian* (New York: Harper & Row Publishers, 1972), p. 145.

2. P.L. Ford, ed., *The Writings of Thomas Jefferson in Arrell Morgan Gibson, The American Indian—Prehistory to Present* (Toronto: D.C. Heath and Company, 1980), p. 271.

3. Arrell Morgan Gibson, *The American Indian—Prehistory to Present* (Toronto: D.C. Heath and Company, 1980), p. 284.

4. Gloria Jahoda, *The Trail of Tears: The Story of the American Indian Removals 1813–1855* (New York: Holt, Rineheart and Winston, 1975), p. 45.

5. Howard Zinn, *A People's History of the United States* (New York: Harper Perennial, 1990), p. 132.

6. John Ehle, *Trail of Tears: The Rise and Fall of the Cherokee Nation* (New York: Anchor Books, Doubleday, 1988), p. 254.

7. Gibson, pp. 322–323.

8. General Scott's address on May 10, 1838, *The Journal of Cherokee Studies 3.3*, 1978, in *Trail of Tears: The Rise and Fall of*

the Cherokee Nation (New York: Anchor Books, Doubleday, 1988), p. 324.

9. Glenn T. Morris, *The State of Native America*, ed. M. Annette Jaimes (Boston: South End Press, 1992), p. 68.

Chapter 6. The Western Tribes

1. Angie Debo, *A History of the Indians of the United States* (Norman, Okla.: University of Oklahoma Press, 1970), p. 126.

2. Herman J. Viola, *After Columbus: The Smithsonian Chronicle of the North American Indian* (Washington, D.C.: Smithsonian Books, 1990), p. 150.

3. *Compton's Encyclopedia*, vol. 3 (Chicago: F.E. Compton, Co., William Benton, Publisher, 1968), p. 362.

4. Joe Starita, *The Dull Knives of Pine Ridge: A Lakota Odyssey* (New York: G.P. Putnam and Sons, 1995), p. 37.

5. Roman Nose, *Touch the Earth: A Self-Portrait of Native American Existence*, ed. T.C. McLuhan (New York: Promontory Press, 1971), p. 88.

6. U.S. Senate, Congressional Record 2462, 46th Congress, 2nd Session (Washington D.C.: U.S. Government Printing Office, 1880) in Glenn T. Morris, *The State of Native America*, ed. M. Annette Jaimes (Boston: South End Press, 1992), p. 67.

7. Peter Press, *A Multicultural Portrait of the Move West* (New York: Marshall Cavendish, 1994), p. 73.

Chapter 7. Life on Reservations

1. Angie Debo, *A History of the Indians of the United States* (Norman, Okla.: University of Oklahoma Press, 1970), p. 238.

2. Vine Deloria, Jr., and Clifford Lytle, *The Nations Within: The Past and Future of American Indian Sovereignty* (New York: Pantheon Books, 1984), p. 9.

3. Arlene Hirschfelder and Martha Kreipe de Montano, *The Native American Almanac* (New York: Prentice Hall General Reference, 1993), p. 16.

4. Sharon O'Brien, *American Indian Tribal Governments* (Norman, Okla.: University of Oklahoma Press, 1989), p. 239.

5. "Lone Wolf Returns . . . To That Long Ago Time," as related by Paul Dyke from his adopted son, *Montana, The Magazine of Western History*, vol. 22, no. 1, January 1972 in Lone Wolf, *Native American Testimony—A Chronicle of Indian-White Relations from Prophecy to the Present, 1492–1992*, ed. Peter Nabokov (New York: Viking, 1991), p. 220.

6. Arrell Morgan Gibson, *The American Indian—Prehistory to Present* (Toronto: D.C. Heath and Company, 1980), p. 434.

7. Walter Echo-Hawk, "Loopholes in Religious Liberty: The Need for Federal Laws to Protect Freedom of Worship for Native People," *Cultural Survival Quarterly*, Winter 1994, pp. 62–65.

8. Ibid.

9. *Some Memories of a Soldier* (New York: Century Company, 1928) in Angie Debo, *A History of the Indians of the United States* (Norman, Okla.: University of Oklahoma Press, 1970), p. 239.

10. Gibson, p. 464.

11. Ibid., p. 479.

12. Ibid.

Chapter 8. Legislation Takes More Native American Land

1. Walter M. Daniels, *American Indians* (New York: The H.W. Wilson Company, 1957), p. 43.

2. Kirke Kickingbird and Karen Ducheneaux, *One Hundred Million Acres* (New York: Macmillan Publishing Company, 1973), p. 16.

3. Walter M. Daniels, *American Indians* (New York: The H.W. Wilson Company, 1957), p. 79.

4. Ibid., p. 78.

5. Arrell Morgan Gibson, *The American Indian—Prehistory to Present* (Toronto: D.C. Heath and Company, 1980), pp. 500–506.

6. Ibid., p. 550.

7. Walter M. Daniels, *American Indians* (New York: The H.W. Wilson Company, 1957), p. 45.

8. Gibson, p. 552.

9. Ibid., p. 556.

10. William T. Hagan, *American Indians: Revised Edition* (Chicago: The University of Chicago Press, 1979), p. 166.

11. Ibid.

Chapter 9. Reservations Today

1. Betty Ballantine and Ian Ballantine, eds., *Native Americans: An Illustrated History* (Atlanta: Turner Publishing, 1993), p. 460.

2. Herman J. Viola, *After Columbus: The Smithsonian Chronicle of the North American Indian* (Washington, D.C.: Smithsonian Books, 1990), p. 278.

3. *Lakota Times*, January 21, 1992 in Jack Utter, *American Indians, Answers to Today's Questions* (Lake Ann, Mich.: National Woodlands Publishing Company, 1993), p. 137.

4. Sar A. Levitan and Elizabeth I. Miller, *The Equivocal Prospects for Indian Reservations* (Arlington, Va.: Public Interest Publications, 1993) in "Tribes Go High-Tech," *The Futurist*, January-February 1994, pp. 48–49..

5. Viola, p. 266.

☆ FURTHER READING ☆

Brown, Dee. *Bury My Heart at Wounded Knee: An Indian History of the American West.* New York: Henry Holt and Company, 1970.

Hakim, Joy. *The First Americans: Prehistory–1600.* New York: Oxford University Press, 2002.

Josephy, Alvin M. Jr. *500 Nations: An Illustrated History of North American Indians.* New York: Knopf, 1994.

Miller, Jay. *Native Americans.* Danbury, Conn.: Children's Press, 1994.

Murdoch, David S. *DK Eyewitness Books: North American Indian.* New York: DK Children, 2005.

☆ INDEX ☆